John Chalmers

The Question of Terms Simplified

Or, the meanings of shan, ling, and ti in Chinese, made plain by induction

John Chalmers

The Question of Terms Simplified
Or, the meanings of shan, ling, and ti in Chinese, made plain by induction

ISBN/EAN: 9783337164232

Printed in Europe, USA, Canada, Australia, Japan

Cover: Foto ©ninafisch / pixelio.de

More available books at **www.hansebooks.com**

THE

QUESTION OF TERMS SIMPLIFIED,

OR

THE MEANINGS OF *SHAN*, *LING*, AND *TI* IN CHINESE MADE PLAIN BY INDUCTION.

.

BY

JOHN CHALMERS, A.M.,
OF THE LONDON MISSIONARY SOCIETY.

CANTON:
E-SHING, PRINTER, SAI-HING-KAI.
HONGKONG: LANE, CRAWFORD & Co.
SHANGHAI: KELLY & WALSH.
1876.

CONTENTS.

Errata.

PAGE 8, LINE 20, FOR is a only   READ is only
„ 14, „ 26, „ (167 *note*)   „   (*P'ei-wan-yun-fu*, char-
                                   acter 性 *passim*)
„ 17, „ 31, „ (259, 317   „   (209—217
„ 23, „ 20, „ *shan*   „   *shan* "
„ 37, „ 30, „ called   „   call

THE QUESTION OF TERMS SIMPLIFIED.

CHAPTER I.

INTRODUCTORY.

It has long appeared to me that the question of terms for God and Spirit in Chinese has been rendered ten-fold more complicated and difficult of settlement than it need be by the manner in which almost every writer has treated it. I by no means plead innocent in this respect. I have felt the temptation to discuss irrelevent topics, and raise side issues, to take advantage of a neighbour's slip at one point, and run off into a dense fog at another, to play in fact at the game of terms, instead of simply trying to elucidate the question in the interests of truth.

Suggestions. At the outset I would throw out a few suggestions for our guidance, the propriety of which will be universally apparent. 1. Let us not raise side issues as if this momentous question were merely a game to be played out between you and me. I am nothing, and my party is nothing, in comparison with the truth in the matter before us. 2. Let us not settle the question by playing off one of our opponents against another, or by quoting one against himself. The *argumentum ad hominem* has been exhausted. We all err at times. 3. Let us not charge each other with dishonesty, or wilful blindness. It is not becoming. "Charity covereth a multitude of sins."

Simplification. The following are some of the ways in which it seems possible to simplify the Question of Terms. 1. A knowledge of "dead languages" is not necessary. Of course I do not mean that an extensive acquaintance with languages ancient and modern, and with Comparative Philology, would not be helpful, but to insist upon such qualifications is only to put off the settlement of the question indefinitely. 2. It is not necessary to read up Egyptian, Babylonian, Greek, Roman, and all other mythologies and cosmogonies. Whether Chinese notions and speech run parallel or contrary to those of any other nation on certain points may be left to be settled afterwards. 3. We may for the most·part steer clear of the higher metaphysics, of ontology and the like, which only a small portion of mankind can enter upon with any satisfaction. 4. Questions as to the grammatical character of the word "God" in our mother-tongue, whether it is generic or particular, absolute or relative, which have puzzled the wisest heads, and still puzzle them, may be left alone. 5. The merits of the question do not turn upon the amount or prevalence of sound theological knowledge among the heathen Chinese. There may be found not a few persons in Christian countries who know little about God besides the name, and superstitious people too who worship images and saints. On the other hand the wisest of us, as Bishop Boone truly said, "can form but very inadequate conceptions of God." But through all the grades of knowledge, from the grossest ignorance up to the inspiration of an apostle, the name holds good for universal use. We may presume that, before the first sentence of the Bible was written, clear notions about creation were not generally prevalent; but we must also presume that among the people for whom it was written "Elohim" meant "God" even before they were aware that He "created the heavens and the earth."

6. Finally a good knowledge of our own Language, and of our English Bible, with sturdy Anglo-Saxon common sense, is all that is needed on the one part, while on the other part the mind must be bent on Chinese *only*, without any foregone conclusions.

Encouragement. I am writing specially for missionaries, and my reason for writing at all just now is because my name has been put forward, without my consent, as a member of a committee on the Question. I write for younger men, at the request of several who take a deep interest in the subject. The older men I cannot presume to instruct. But to the young men who "are strong," I say, Come to the consideration of this subject free from foregone conclusions. Do not settle the question *a priori;* and do not suppose that it is settled for you. *It is not settled.* And it is a shame and a reproach to the whole missionary body that it remains as it is. Do not content yourselves with the trite remark that there is much to be said on both sides. This is only another device of the enemy for putting off the happy day of union. It is just as incumbent on the young man who arrives in the field to-day to set about settling this question, as it was incumbent on

Boone or Medhurst, Williams or Legge. That they and their contemporaries and successors did not settle it, and have not settled it, only makes apparent the necessity of some change of method. You have to thank them for much ; though indeed it is not strange if you feel at times inclined to blame them for this. Nevertheless they have by their labours placed you on a vantage-ground from which you can attack the difficulty with far better prospects of overcoming it than they had. They have facilitated wonderfully the acquisition of Chinese, so that you can with comparative ease learn to read the context of passages where the, as yet, unknown terms occur. Let these be to you as x, y, z,—unknown quantities. Then by the help of those who have gone before you, get the ability to read *purely native literature* without referring to a teacher or a Dictionary at every point. Let all foreign-made Chinese books, all versions of the Bible, all Tracts and Treatises on Christianity, be to you non-existent as far as this question is concerned. Their evidence, so long as it is self-contradictory, is null.

Chinese Idiom. The field of Chinese literature is of vast extent and highly cultivated. Whatever may be thought of Chinese style or idiom, it is a thing established. We might as well expect to change the course of nature, as to change the idiom or usage of the Chinese Language. Paul and the other writers of the New Testament did not violently change the usages of the Greek Language, and if they had sought to do so they could not have succeeded ; for even to this day their style is tested, and approved or condemned, by the standard of classic Greek; or, if not that, at least it is tried by the previously existing standard of the Hellenistic dialect. But if any one thinks that the appreciation and the influence of classic or cultivated style in Chinese is evanescent, and may be disregarded, let him reflect upon the esteem in which classic Greek and Latin, that is heathen Greek and Latin, are held even at the present day after eighteen centuries of Christian culture; and let him reflect again, that the hold which Chinese Literature has upon this great people is immensely greater than that which either Greek or Latin had upon the nations of Europe at the beginning of the Christian era. Christianity did not kill out the taste for classic Greek and Latin, and he is a bold prophet who says that Christianity, even with western civilization, railways, and telegraphs super-added, is going to crush out Chinese Literature. Whoever acts on such a supposition is not wise.

Method. The field of Chinese Literature, as I have said, is immense; and I do not profess to have explored a tithe of it; but only to have made incursions into it here and there, where varieties of subject and of style invited. As a preparation for the present essay, I have, in the course of a few weeks, made a selection from a small and imperfect library, with the occasional help of the *P'ei-wan-yun-fu*, of nearly 600 passages tending to throw light on the meaning and usage of the *Terms.* When the point to be established was important, or one on which there exists difference of opinion, I selected many examples, and where no difference of opinion exists, I was content with one or two just to complete the view of native usage. It

must therefore be distinctly understood, that a multitude of examples of one use of a word does not, *unless so stated*, signify that as many examples could
not be found of another, where only one or two are
given. I have no notion of securing the preference
for one common usage to the rejection of another
that is also common, by a triumphant production of
one or two hundred more examples. The curious
question whether Dr. Williams gives most examples
of *shan* for " god " or of *shan* for " spirit " does not
tend to good. The Chinese tradesman hangs up a
lantern at his shop door every day with " reverence
shan " on it, and there are perhaps few days on which
he does not make some remark about his own or another's *tsing-shan*, " good spirit." How can we decide the case by a majority of instances, when, on
both sides, they are numerous as the sand? The
List of examples and quotations from native books I
have decided to print as an Appendix, and they are
numbered for convenience of reference. I shall always give the number of each sentence referred to in
the subsequent pages, so that the reader may turn to
it at once. There is a certain order and method
aimed at in this List, which will appear from the
English headings, but if individual sentences seem
here and there out of place, it must not be supposed
that the force of my argument is dependent on the
arrangement, so that finding some fault with that
would upset it.

Weighing evidence. As to the comparative value
of evidence on the immediate points at issue, I place
(1) first, the usage of well-known and approved Chinese writers, (2) next, the definitions given in native
books, (3) third, the observations of good foreign

Sinologists, and (4) last of all, what native teachers who know our views may tell us. Definitions in native books, especially in philosophical books, sometimes conflect with usage, and with one another, in which case they are of little or no value. Foreign definitions may be used to confirm an inference from native usage, but are utterly worthless on the opposite side; and taken by themselves are of little account. A good native teacher is a valuable assistant so long as he does not know one's motive for consulting him; but the moment he knows his employer's motives and wishes, he is the most prejudiced of all witnesses. He is ingeniously untruthful. Colloquial usage, unless where the colloquial is in print and of strictly Chinese origin, belongs to the third or fourth class of evidence. At best it is but hearsay or second-hand.

Arguments involving two or three logical steps, and drawn from single definitions of several words found *anywhere*, are not only feeble, but often vicious, or else ridiculous.

CHAPTER II.

WHAT WE WANT.

Spirit. In the English Language the word
Spirit, as regards its variety of meanings, may be
compared to the word Light. 1. Light is *something* belonging to and forming an integral part of
something else; as, "the light of the sun." 2.
Light is simply a quality, in which sense it is
either an adjective or a substantive (=bright or
brightness); as, "a light and airy room," "a thing
of light and life." 3. A Light is something
luminous (=a luminary, a taper); as, "God made
two great lights," "he called for a light." This
usage is called metonymy. 4. Light is spoken of
as a distinct essence; as "God said, Let there be
light, and there was light." Then, in this sense,
Light is a subject of science, and there are two
theories about it; according to the *corpuscular
theory* it is really an independent essence; but
according to the *undulatory theory* it is a only a
quality or condition of undulation of something
else called a *medium.* If the former theory be true
the more scientific meaning of light is the first.
Light is then a *thing.* If the latter theory be the
correct one, then the second meaning is the more
correct, or scientific. Light then is a *quality.*

The analogy between the above and what follows is almost complete; and the reader will excuse

me, if he does not thank me, as we proceed, for being a little particular about this illustration. We will suppose that the account of Light is understood and admitted. Then, we go on to give the plan of this essay.

I. A SPIRIT is something belonging to and forming an integral part of a living being; as " the Spirit of God", "the spirit of man"; in which sense the word is more or less personal.

II. SPIRIT is simply a quality; as, "a man of spirit;" in which sense it is not personal.

III. A SPIRIT is a spiritual being; as "God is a spirit" (which expression becomes altered in all our minds to "God is pure spirit"), "they supposed that they had seen a spirit," " Sir Spirit, I doubt I do nick-name you, for those of your kind (they say) have no sense" (sensation. *Queen Elizabeth to Lord Burleigh)*, "several energetic spirits resident at Amoy" *(China Mail)*. This usage is, strictly speaking, what is called metonymy. The whole Being, the entire person, is included in the word which primarily denotes only a part.

IV. SPIRIT is spoken of as a distinct essence; as, "The Egyptians are men and not God; their horses are flesh and not spirit." This usage directly suggests the inquiry, "What is spirit?" And then we have as before, in the case of Light, two theories, the one, that spirit is really a distinct essence, in which case the philosophical account of it approaches to the first meaning; the other, that it is only a mood, or mode of activity of matter, which approaches to the second meaning. Here we come on the verge of higher metaphysics, a land of extreme indefiniteness, and interminable mists. Spirit becomes either personal or impersonal, and we cannot tell in many cases which sort is meant. From each of the above leading meanings there branch off any number of different shades of meaning and figurative uses. "Spirit" has 21 meanings in *Webster*, and "Light" has 26. I mention this only to make it more clear that they belong to the same class of words. We have at present little to do with the figurative meanings, and we shall deal only with the broader distinctions here pointed out, chiefly under the three following heads.

I. *Soul and Spirit.* The word "soul", seems primarily to coincide with "spirit" in the first sense as referring to man, but only to man, and in its secondary uses it is much more restricted than "spirit." Whether "the soul of man" is identical with "the spirit of man" is an open question. It must be admitted however that the soul, if not a different thing from the spirit, is the same thing viewed in a different aspect. The idea of spirit is decidedly finer or purer, and more subtile than that of soul; and whether we accept the tripartition of human nature into "body soul and spirit" or not, we cannot dispense with either word in this connection. The German missionaries, if they do not all hold the doctrine of tripartition, are all so familiar with it that they probably never fail to seek at an early period for the best terms by which to express "soul and spirit" in Chinese.

As there is no controversy about the word for soul, I may state here that *hwun* (36) alone (not *ling-hwun*) is the word almost invariably used in Chinese for the soul of the living. The other word *p'oh* (40) presents a still grosser conception with which nothing in our language coincides. We may for distinctions sake call it the "shade." But in our systems of psychology the word is superfluous. The combination *ling-hwun* (222-224) is also sanctioned by usage but not common. We shall return to this by and by.

II. *Spirituality, Genius, Intellect.* The three words, spirituality, genius, and intellect (intelligence,) all denote uncommon or *variable* qualities of the heart or mind and come under our second meaning of spirit. The first is primarily the most comprehensive, referring to the affections, the emotions, the tastes, and the thoughts. It is now, however, much confined to a religious use, and refers specially to the affections. Genius (not the personified Latin *Genius*) has generally no reference to the affections. In other respects it is much the same as the first. Intellect or intelligence refers only to the tastes and thoughts, and says nothing about the affections or the emotions. In religious teaching we want especially the equivalent of the first of these words.

III. *God, gods, spirits.* The word "God" whether it be in the singular or in the plural, manifestly does not belong to the same class with the words "Light" and "Spirit," which have so many and divers meanings and shades of meaning. "God" is held rigidly to one sense, and the only real distinction is that of "true God" and "false god." The question "What is God?" is also of a different nature from "What is spirit?" The former does not take us directly and unavoidably into the domain of metaphysics. There is one step remaining, and by that one step Theology *may* pass into metaphysics ; or she may save herself and wisely stop short after replying,

" God is a Spirit." Although the definition of
" god" specially adopted by one side in the discussion
before us, " a worshipped *being*," is novel and faulty,
" God" is certainly either the name of a *Being*, or of
only *one* class of *beings*, under our third meaning of
" spirit." All spirits are not gods. When taken as
the name of a class (generically, if you please)—
"god," "gods"—it is like "luminary" under the word
"Light." All lights are not luminaries. Luminary
is soon defined : it is a light of heaven :—the sun,
moon, and stars are luminaries. We define it by
saying, " It is a light." But the ulterior question
" What is light ?" is of a different sort. It takes
a great deal of science to answer that. So we can
define " God" as above, but we cannot go a step
farther and define "spirit." Let this be distinctly
understood and borne in mind. *The word " God"*
is outside of pure metaphysics. The word "Spirit" is
inside of pure metaphysics. We define God to be a
Spirit, and if our definition is accepted there is no
more to be said. But the ulterior question "What
is a Spirit ?" perplexes us. We simply cannot
answer it. And it is around this word that the
battles of metaphysics have to be fought over and
over again without end. We must accept the existence of spirit as an *ultimate fact.* Our analysis
can go no further. To say, " Spirit is God, or
such a being as God, or angel, or man," is to sound
a retreat. You then evidently give it up.

If we select a word which means " spirit " and
use it for " God " we put the *ultimate idea* (spirit)
in the place of the *penultimate* (god); and leave it
no longer possible to say " God is a Spirit." We
can only say " Spirit is Spirit " (490).

CHAPTER III.

FIRST SENSE OF SPIRIT—*SHAN.*

Shan stands at the head of this chapter by virtue of its prevalent use, as will be understood by glancing over the first 200 examples in the Appendix. *Ling* occurs a few times, but its meaning is as yet indefinite. With *shan* it is different ; we can ascertain its meaning from the multitude of examples, quite near enough to the truth for all practical purposes. I know there is a theory that *shan* ought not to be used for " spirit " but exclusively for " God ", " gods "; but we have nothing to do with any theory just now. It will perhaps appear as we proceed with our examination of facts that *shan* is legitimately as well as habitually used by the best Chinese writers for "spirit"; and, if so, I have already pointed out that such a habitual usage cannot be abolished by any power on earth. Moreover it is extremely undesirable, even in a theological point of view, to abolish this usage, because it will presently appear to us all, if I am not very much mistaken, that there is no other word in the language that comes near answering to "spirit." *Shan* of course only approximates in all its usages to the English word. It is probably true that *no two words either in the same language or in different languages are perfectly synonymous.* We should remember this. And I have one other general

remark to make, namely, that it is not necessarily
any desecration of a word that is used for " God "
or " gods ", nor need it be reckoned a sin or a
heathenish error, to use it at the same time with an
entirely different reference. All depends on the
nature of the word. I may call a man " the Lord",
though I must not call him " God." And how
are we to discover the nature of a word except by
inquiring for what purpose it is used ? I do not mean
to deify the man whom I call " my Lord ", nor does
the Chinese mean to deify himself when he says " my
spirit is high " (183). The theory referred to takes
another shape, namely, that etymologically the word
shan contains in it the idea of divinity. But if any
part of the etymological contents of a word is entirely
lost, it is to all intents and purposes the same as if
it had never been there. In the expression just quoted,
shan-kau " high spirit ", or, according to English
idiom, "high spirits", there is ever present the mystic,
metaphysical idea described in last chapter, but not
a trace of *divinity*.

    Shan emotional. I find in the Chinese Language
feelings of pleasure and pain, emotions of fear, sorrow,
joy, excitement, and the like, ascribed to the *sin* (63),
heart or mind, to the *hwun* (36), soul, and to the
sing (167 *note*), nature. I seek for another word
which in common usage takes turns with these in
representing that sensitive, emotional, excitable *something* that is within us all. Other words like *p'oh*
(64), shade, *k'i*, air (impersonal, spiritual substance,
524) may be found as the subject of emotions, but
they are rejected by common consent as unfit to re-
present "spirit." *Tsing*, essence (alone 58, 81, 86,
not in combination as *tsing-shan*) and *ling* (alone

73, 82, 119, not in combination as *sing-ling)* are sometimes the subject of *motions*, but not of feelings or *emotions* in a living man. I have been particular about *ling* in this connection, and have faithfully put down whatever tended to illustrate the use of the word. There is just one instance of *ling* (alone 167) being " pleased "; but it is a sort of exception which greatly confirms the rule. In the first place, the passage copied verbatim from the *P'ei-wan-yun-fu* is in all respects so obscure that, without a reference to the *History of Han* from which it is taken, it is impossible to punctuate it; and in the second place, it is thought necessary to add a note of explanation, that " pleasing *ling* means pleasing the emotional and intelligent nature." *Sing-ling* is a well established combination (35, 158). *Ling* is therefore perhaps used elliptically for *sing-ling*.* In the latter passage quoted (158) the reason for adding *ling* to *sing*, nature, is stated to be that man's nature is most *ling*, intelligent, and thus a contrast is brought out between " nature", and " stupefaction " by drink.

If hereafter a case can be made out for *ling* as signifying the spirit of a living human being, either in the sense of the fluctuating " animal spirits " or of the emotional spirit common to all men, which " returns to God who gave it " or "goes upward " at death (226—228), what I am now saying in behalf of *shan* for " spirit " may be so far set aside, but not otherwise. I do not simply *say* what follows, I hold up before the eyes of readers who know Chinese the *facts*. The *shan* of a living human being is capable

---

* Referring to the original it appears that " pleasing-*ling* " was really a name of a rank in the emperor's harem,="pleasers of his majesty ".

of suffering, is frequently wounded or broken (1—16), toiled, weary, or sorrowful, in bitterness, or in affliction (17—38). It may be sick (39). It may be frightened or stunned (41—54), bewildered, foolish, or besotted (21,54—62). It is sometimes stirred by feelings of pity, wonder, longing, or impatience (63—72). At other times it wanders in dreams, fancy, reverie, or madness (74—80). It may be wasted, or squandered by dissipation or over-work (83). But again it is restored, quieted, comforted, brightened, made free (84—129). It is occupied and attentive (130—138). It is then cared for, cultivated, refreshed, solemnized, or harmonized. or has tone given to it (139—164.) It has emotions of joy, being elevated, elated, or even overflowing with pleasurable excitement and eagerness (166—186, 209).

It will perhaps be noticed that among the above instances, which all refer to living men and women, nothing of a strictly moral character or of affection, as love or hatred, is ascribed to *shan;* but a reference to *Cruden's Concordance* will show that the same is the case with "spirit". Words like "bad", "good", "love", "hate", are rarely if ever used in speaking of the human spirit. Such terms are reserved for other kinds of spirits which we shall come to by and by. Where we say "a man has a bad spirit" (disposition), the Chinese would probably not use *shan* (*but see* 193).

Shan-ming (135, 199—208, 513). I have put down over ten examples of *shan-ming* is connection with the spirits of the living, though the sense is often that of a special quality, in order to call attention to the fact that this combination is far from being the exact equivalent of "the gods". It is

necessary in every case to observe the connection before even loosely translating it by any term denoting
objects of worship. The first sentence is from *Chu-
tsze on Mind*, and he says. "From first to last the
mind in its constitution and function, though there are
contained in it, it may be, both what is true and what
is false, both what is right and what is wrong, is in real-
ity all alike the mystery of *shan-ming* inscrutable."
Must we always bring in "the gods" in such cases as
this ? or, does not the philosopher rather mean the inscrutable mystery of spirit which has been already
pointed out ? Here is another sentence (204):—"The
ears and eyes attend to their own duties, and the *shan-
ming* keeps its dwelling" *i.e.* the spirit keeps its place
within (537). I am not going to translate all the
passages, but please look at them, my brethren, before you make up your minds irrevocably that *shan-
ming* is equivalent to "the gods". Can the shadow
of a reason be given for not translating this term by
"spiritual intelligence", singular or plural as the
case may be ? If we do so it becomes at once evident how it is that the Chinese worship the "spiritual
intelligences" that are outside or above them, and
at the same time have "spiritual intelligence" within.
*Worshipping a being does not alter the nature of the
word used to indicate that being.* In the last sentence quoted (208) the mystic word has received, as
often it does, a more mystic explanation, upon which
the laconic remark of my Chinese assistant is "The
more explained, the less understood".

    Tsing-shan (259, 317, 228—231, 474, 509,
513, 514, 516, 526). Of all combinations of *shan* and
another character probably *tsing-shan* is the most
common. Yet it is not so very common in books as

its constant use in colloquial might lead us to expect. I have a few remarks to make on this expression, all of which are justified by the Chinese quotations. 1. *Tsing-shan* and *shan* alone, when used for the spirits of human beings, are in general the same. The former term is a little more vague in form than the latter, owing to the extreme ambiguity of *tsing*, but this is compensated for by the distinction which it serves to make between the human spirit and other spirits. The addition of a syllable which means almost anything or nothing (essence, subtilty, fine, &c.) becomes useful in this way. 2. Both terms, *shan* and *tsing-shan*, vary in meaning from the most concrete and personal sense of soul, to that of a mere feeling of health and animation which we call "good spirits." 3. In this last sense, the usual colloquial one, *tsing* serves the purpose of a qualifying adjective, as in example (213) where the writer "Arose from sleep and felt in good spirits." Here *tsing-shan* is like *shan-kau* "in high spirits" (182, 183). 4. *Tsing-shan* is used for the spirit after death as well as before (228—231, 514). *Chu-tsze* says, the *tsing-shan* goes up as an "air" to heaven (474). But he says elsewhere that *tsing* is the "shade" and *shan* is the soul, and that the former goes downward, and the latter upward at death (519—521). So then, according to Chu-tsze, *tsing-shan* may be either one thing, namely, a human spirit that goes upward to God; or two very different things with different destinies. "Who knoweth?" *(Eccl.* III. 21.)

Shan of the dead. I have acted on the suggestion of Confucius (See *Analects* XI. 11.), and taken up first what we know most about, the living. We have seen what place *shan* holds in the living man. When he dies the same usage continues uninterruptedly. At the moment of death, it is the *shan* that passes away (218). Immediately the *shan* returns to its original source (221), or the *shan* ascends to the ninth heavens (226). Bereaved friends however see the *shan* of the dead in their dreams and have converse with them (233, 235). Sometimes the *shan* can be summoned back by magic art (237). Sometimes the dead come of their own accord in bodily shape and tell that their *shan* are not at rest (239). Observe all this is quite independent of, and antecedent in the order of nature to, any peculiar custom of sacrificing to the dead. Whatever remains of activity or life without distinction of class or character is called *shan* (420, 522). As remarked above, it is also called *tsing-shan*. According to the school of Chu-tsze, it is just the *tsing-shan* of the dead that their descendants are supposed to worship (526). I say " supposed " because it is painfully evident that Chu-tsze encourages the sham worship of beings that he does not believe have any personal or conscious existence (228, 521, 523, 528, 556). Observe that he admits a sort of " air ", which is euphoniously called the *tsing-shan* of king Wan, to have gone up and united with Heaven (474), but in reference to the suggestion of a more spiritual man than himself, that something of immortality belongs to us all, he says, " It cannot be intended that when we die we, so to speak, have *tsing-ling* that does not perish." *Tsing-ling* is different from *tsing-shan*, which may be anything

resembling the spirit of wine (318). *Tsing-ling*
means intelligence, and implies consciousness or
at least individuality (259—263, 575). It is
strange, after reading some of the dissertations of
the orthodox on the proper way to keep the balance
even between wisdom (conviction?) on the one hand
which says the dead they worship are no more, and
benevolence on the other which will not hold them
dead (513), to read the statement of the same men
that one of the peculiarities of the Buddhist creed,
just then imported from India, is that "when men
die their *tsing-shan* does not become extinct" (514).
I may here call attention to two very bold statements
by members of the same orthodox school, whose
ideal man is *chi-ch'ing* "most sincere" (!). One
says that "the ideal men when he offers sacrifice
need not believe in the existence of any *shan* in
heaven or on earth that he sacrifices to. He does it
solely for example and instruction" (532). Another
says, "There is Air above, Form below, and Knowledge in the middle. These are the three Powers.
Air is a ghost, *kwei*, is not that Heaven? Knowledge is a spirit, *shan*, is not that man? It is we that
have get the rational nature" (482). With such
passages before me, am I not justified in regarding
with some suspicion the spiritual definitions of philosophical Books?

There are other names for the portion of a man
that survives or outlasts the body. *Hwun*, soul, is
retained and of course *p'oh*, shade. It is here that
the latter comes into play, either, (A) as a separate
entity, when it is an unquestionable *kwei*, or ghost,
a dark, cold, and injurious being (519, 521, 518),
but usually returns soon like the body to the dust

(521, 522) ; or, (B) in union with the *hwun*, when the dissolution is not complete as in the case of sudden death on the battle field. Then "the spirit retains its consciousness and faculties in full vigour, and the *hwun-p'oh* being resolute becomes a brave ghost" (579). "Ghosts", *kwei*, is the name which is distinctive for the spirits of the dead as different from the spirits of the living *(shan)*, from the spirit of Heaven that liveth and abideth for ever *(shan)*, and the spirit of the Earth which is otherwise distinguished *(k'i)*. But Heaven, Earth, and living man, all three alike, have what is called *shan*. Neither of them is strictly speaking a *shan*, but all three have *shan* (525). Put this in plain English with "god" for *shan*. "Heaven has a god, Earth has a god, and living man has a god ; only when man dies his god is called a ghost." Surely if ever a word was out of place "god" is out of place here. For "god" read "spirit", and all is plain.

The concrete use of *ling* for the relics or emblems, as well as for the souls, of the dead, will be explained in another chapter. It may however be said in general that, while *kwei* means death and extinction, "a dying ghost", *shan* means a living spirit (522), and *ling* attributes consciousness and intelligence to the dead (513).

Our Spirits. "My *shan*", "his *shan*", "your *shan*" mean invariably "my spirit", "his spirit", "your spirit" in Chinese books (2, 11, 12, 13, 15, 22, 33, 34, 52, 55, 59, 63, 85, 114, 115, 126, 150, 171, 178, 192, 196, 217, 237, 239, 240). What I intend to say is that, wherever a personal name or pronoun in the possessive case precedes *shan*, this word does not mean the person's object of worship

outside, but his own spirit within which belongs to
no body else. Of course, as in English "my spirit"
might have the meaning of "my God" *forced* upon
it, or it might mean among spiritualists the attend-
ant spirit that is always hovering about me, so in
Chinese. The one language is just as plastic in this
respect as the other, and, I suppose, no more. One
can tell from the connection of your discourse that
you do not mean your own spirit, but the one you
were just speaking of as having something to do with
you.* But thus far the authority of native usage is
entirely wanting for "my *shan*" in the sense of
"my God."

Having made it plain beyond a doubt that "the
shan of a man" is his spirit; it follows as a matter
of course that "the *shan* of *Ti*," whether this word be
Jove or God, means also His spirit (488).

---

* But let the reader try the experiment of asking any unpreju-
diced Chinese the meaning of Isaiah viii. 19. with *ki-chi-shan* for
"their God."

CHAPTER IV.

SECOND SENSE OF SPIRIT—*LING* AND *SHAN*.

When denoting a quality, *ling* and *shan* are both used either as substantives or adjectives.

1. The highest style of man, the *shing-jan*, who is perfect according to the Chinese ideal, and is more than a genius, is described as *shan* (497—502). *Ling* seems inadequate to express inward perfection. In this connection I recommend to the attention of the reader the remarks of Yang-tsze-yun on *shan*, as genius or spiritual penetration (502).

2. The genius of a painter or poet is called *shan*, (241, 242, 284, 287). The same thing is called *ling* (243). In either case the idea is special powers of mind, taste and skill, or ability. *Shan* however is the most common word in the sense of genius. It is often said of a writer, or of a person of extraordinary ability, "He does this as if he had *shan*, that is, as if he had a genius within him. "*Shan*-help" is equivalent to poetic *inspiration*. Nobody thinks of asking, who helps, or who inspires? To have caught the *shan* of another (289) is precisely the same idea as that in the following lines :—

"A perfect judge will read each work of wit'
"With the same spirit that its author writ."

Different from this usage is *ju-shan*, "like a spirit," which is a comparison, as in the following

sentence :— " Like spirits they" (the wise men)
" came casting no shadow before them, and like
spirits they departed passing away into the obscurity
from which they had emerged" *(Dr Hanna)*.

3. Persons have the quality of *shan* or of *ling*
ascribed to them for a variety of reasons of a lower
nature than the actual possession of sage perfection
or genius. Here we come to the most common use
of *ling*. *Shan* is still preferred in certain connections, where mystery is a leading idea ; as when the
awe-inspiring reserve of kings is spoken of, which
indeed is considered equivalent to the possession of
genius, on the ground of *omne ignotum pro magnifico*.
" Authority is the *shan* (soul) of the king " (275).
" Propriety and righteousness are the *shan* (soul)
of a prince" (276). Expressions like "*shan*-courage-"
(312, 313) and " *shan*-steed " (314) may be inter-
preted either by " spirited " or " spirit-like "; but in
any case *shan* here departs far from the sense of
ling. A " *ling* horse " would be as different as possible from a " *shan* horse." The former would perhaps denote a horse with supernatural or unusual
intelligence, but the latter denotes a horse of extraordinary swiftness.

4. *Ling.* Let us now take leave of *shan* for a
time and concentrate our attention on *ling*. In
frequency of use and variety of meanings this word
is subordinate to *shan*. It does not occur very often
in the classics. We shall give here all the cases
we find in Dr Legge's published *Volumes*, including
the *Tso-chuen*, and avail ourselves of the *Translation*
to bring out the meaning. The references will enable
any one to consult the original. Of course a translation must be such as to make sense. The reader

may try to substitute the word spirit in each case, for Dr. Legge's translation of *ling*, and judge if it will fit, especially if it will fit in the sense of "soul and spirit", for no other would be of any avail.

For antiquity and *genuineness*, anything that comes down in the form of poetry* ought always to be preferred to prose; it has something like organic life in it. Let us therefore begin with the *Book of Poetry*, or, as it has been otherwise well named, the "Old Ballad Book". The *Translator's* equivalent for *ling* will be always put in italics.

Ling in the Book of Poetry. "When the *good* rains had fallen" I. iv. VI. 2. "The *marvellous* tower". "The *marvellous* park". "The *marvellous* pond" III. i. VIII. The child came in to the world without giving any pain "shewing how *wonderful* he would be" (the first cultivator of grain). III. ii. I. 2. "Glorious was his fame; brilliant, his *energy*." (Woo-ting's). IV. iii. V. 5.

Ling in the Book of History. "I did not slight your plans, I only used what were *best* of them". IV. vii. Pt. iii. 7. "Of all creatures man is the most *highly endowed*. The sincere, intelligent, and perspicacious among men becomes the great sovereign". V. i. Pt. i. 2. [*Chinese Note* (539). "Intelligent is also *ling*. The sage possesses before me that of which I have the seeds in common with himself, and among *intelligent beings (ling)* he is the most *intelligent (ling)*".]. "The sovereigns of our Chow for their great *goodness* were charged with the work of God." V. xiv. 13. "The first cause of his evil course was his internal misrule which made him unfit to deal *well* with the multi-

---

* See *Note B* at the end of this essay.

tudes "; but, "Our kings of Chow treated *well* the multitudes ". V. xviii. 5. 9. "Among the people of Meau, they did not use the *power of good*, but the restraints of punishments ". V. xxvii. 3.

Ling in the Tso-chuen. "By the *good influence* of his lordship, I have no serious hurt ". V. 28. " I venture to depend on your *powerful imfluence*, to complete the victory of my army ". VII. 12. " I will remember your *kindness.* VIII. 3. "By the *powerful influence* of your ruler I find myself", a stranger, safe among you. VIII. 16. "The marquis of Ts'e invaded Lae, the people of which sent to bribe the chief eunuch of Ts'e with a hundred choice horses and as many oxen. On this the army of Ts'e returned. From this the reader "might know that " the above marquis "was indeed *ling* " (*Ling* was his posthumous title). IX. 3. The continued success of certain negotiations " is to be ascribed to your lordship's *powerful influence.*" IX. 11. " If by your " (his ministers') " *influence*'" I come to die a natural death, pray, call me after-wards, "*Ling* (562), or *Le* (223)." IX. 13. " If by your" (his ministers') " *powerful influence* I preserve my head and neck, &c." X. 25. " Now I wish by the blessing and *powerful influence* of king Ch'ing to repair the walls, &c." Ch'ing had built the walls some centuries before.' X. 32. My ruler now wishes to seek the blessing of the duke of Chow, and desires to beg the *help of the power* of the Tsang family." XII. 24.

There is nothing in the *Four Books* to be added to these examples of the use of *ling ;* and in all probability the radical meanings of the word are exhausted as far as it is applied to living men.

Let us take them in the order in which they occur.

(A) "Good," "best," "goodness," "well," "the power of good," "good influence," "kindness":—these all suggest a powerful leaning of the word to virtue's side, so to speak; and there is no mistake about it, for the commentaries and Dictionaries quite agree that *ling* has the meaning of "good" (561); the first example from the *Poetry* requires some meaning of the kind, "rains" in their season can only be good, kindly, useful rains; and most of the other phrases are complimentary, amounting to "by your favour", though stronger than that. But the evidence that "good" is an essential part of the meaning of *ling*, and not an occasional or metaphoric sense put upon it, is that when it is used in a concrete way, that is to denote the being of which it is a quality, it is never qualified further by an adjective meaning either good or bad. A good *ling* would be a tautology, and a bad *ling* would be a contradiction in terms. There are certainly no "bad *ling*" or "evil *ling*" in native books. Nothing immoral or malignant is ever imputed to a *ling*. I cannot produce evidence of this, and must content myself with asking those who think otherwise, or adopt another usage, to produce their authority. But now, granting that "good" is an inseparable element in the meaning of *ling*, I here observe further that neither "spirit" nor *shan* has any such element of good in it; and on this we have, on the one hand the evidence of *Webster's Dictionary*, and on the other the passages quoted in the Appendix (443—463). Thus far then *shan* coincides with "spirit," and *ling* is different from both.

(B) "Marvellous", "wonderful":—these expressions must be elliptical, and we must supply the quality, either "goodness" or some of those that follow, which excites marvel or wonder. At first sight this seems to resemble a meaning of *shan* which is well known, "inscrutable"; but there is perhaps no respect in which the antithesis of the two words comes out more strikingly than in this. In ancient times there were towers called " *ling* towers", and others, it seems, called " *shan* towers". The difference is explained with reference to the men that had them built. The one *(shan)* resembled heaven in its intrinsic depth, the other *(ling)* resembled earth in its superficial adornment (550)—he was "a remarkable man ". In this respect, heaven, however bright it may be to look at, corresponds to *(yiu)* the obscure and unfathomable which is *shan*, and earth corresponds to (*ming*) the bright and intelligible which is *ling* (551). In a metaphysical point of view, *shan* must always take the precedence of *ling* (563), because it expresses the profoundest mystery of spirituality. It is specially the attribute of sages, perfect men, who are supposed to be in intimate communion with the universal Spirit (552—556). But it is also an attribute of every man. Even the most foolish (251) and the most depraved (199), that is those who have least *ling*, and creatures lower in the scale than man also (520, 530), are *shan*, and have a *shan* in them. And there is not a shadow of blasphemy or heresy in this, viewed in the light of the Bible; because *shan* is not and can never be the same sort of word that "god" is. Do we not read of the "spirit of the beast that goeth downward to the earth"? And is that not a mystery? It is surely

a thing unfathomable. And it is a widely different
thing from the marvellous sagacity *(ling)* displayed
by some of those beasts, as apes for example (568).
This is *ling*, and it is contrasted with the stupidity
of other animals. But *shan* is life, fire, spirit (539—
544). . A horse that in swiftness seems to fly and not
touch the ground is a *shan*-horse (314), also marvellous in his way, but different from the apes. He
has spirit. The Chinese would not describe him as
ling. A soldier who never turns his back on the
enemy, but cuts his way through their ranks, has
shan-courage (312, 313). So we should say, "he
has *spirit*". And the Chinese would no more think
of describing him as having *ling*, than we should of
praising his sagacity or intelligence, or his kindly
disposition. Look at that poor pheasant eagerly
pecking up grains of food along the meadow till
suddenly it treads on a snare and is caught. Its
spirit (*shan*) was in full force, but it was "not good"
(184). No more is that man's high spiritual condition good who has drunk a hundred cups at a sit-
ting (185); or that of the other, who audaciously
plunges into a swollen stream and attempts to swim
across it (186). All these have *shan*, but with a
deficiency of *ling*.

(C) "Energy" is the translation given of *ling*
is one passage in the *Book of Poetry*. "Energy"
is closely allied to courage. But of course it is
mental energy that is meant, or else "powerful influence" as in other passages. "There is no spiritual excitement imputed, though of course it is im-
plied, by *ling*, when denoting" "influence" or "mental effort". "Pure intellect" (*hü-ling*, 573, 574,
575) would not likely manifest any "power" or "in

fluence '. There is is always a spirit behind, that is, an emotional nature; and every manifestation of *ling*, is an effect of *shan*, as *ling* itself is a quality of the *shan* or soul. This is very much the difference between the words; *shan* is a cause, *ling* is an effect.'

(D) " Highly endowed ", " intelligent ".—Here we come to one of the household words of China, " Man is the *ling* of all things "; and *ling* has the current colloquial meaning, for the phrase in the *Book of History* and the colloquial usage are inseparably connected. *Tsing-ling* ("smart, apt, clever ". *Williams),* *ming-ling* ("smart intelligent, quick of apprehension ". *Ib.*), *ling-pien* (" quick at perceiving," " the pith of a machine ". *Ib.*), are expressions about which there is no mistake. Does a Chinese student then understand when he reads the sentence, " But man of all things is *ling*", that man is here said to be "spiritual"* above all things ? We know that " smartness" is an effect of spirit, but it is a very outward and visible sign, having a very remote connection with any inward and spiritual grace. I am not trifling. I mean what I say; and I beg my brethren to reflect upon it. We want to speak about the most inward and vital things, about the heart and affections, and the spirit of a man which is the candle of the Lord; and shall we set aside *shan*, the only word in the language which seems to penetrate the inmost soul of a man (502) in favour of an outward, obvious, unmysterious term like *ling* ? Do not the commentators tell us that *ling* here is equivalent to the two words, "intelligent and perspicacious ", which immediately follow ? And do we get any

---

* In a Tract on the *Name of God in Chinese* which I published 13 years ago, I translated *ling* by "spiritual;" but there is reason to doubt this rendering, though in a loose way of speaking *shan* and *ling* are interchanged.

nearer to the mystery of our being, when we reflect upon the sage being the " most intelligent of human intelligences"? (557). How very different in tendency from this is the expression of Chwang-tsze, referring to the same class of men, but gazing inward upon their souls, "they are the spiritual among spirits", and as a result of this they "are capable of more subtilty" than others! (500). Or take the following, and here I present to the friends of *chishan* for God a far better *part* of a sentence than any that has been produced hitherto on that side: " There is a Perfect Spirit in heaven, who is the Lord of creation ; and the spirit of the sage" (our word for saint) " is the fountain of truth. The Spirit is one " (367). Whatever defects of doctrine any one may discover in this "form of words", the words we want are unmistakeably here. Compare, "But he that is joined unto the Lord is one Spirit". 1 Cor. VI. 17.

(E) " Influence", " powerful influence ".—Most readers must have begun to suspect that the word *ling* in Chinese covers a wider ground than any English word we can translate it by. Such is undoubtedly the case. We cannot even put the above meanings into one phrase, much less express them all in one word. If we call it "good intellectual and perceptive abilities", or more vaguely "good abilities", the notions of "marvellous" and of "influence" are excluded. Sometimes the Greek word *nous* has been introduced into this discussion, but *nous* " mind", "thought", "intelligence", is far too narrow for *shin ;* and at the same time, too concrete for *ling*. We speak of " keeping a thing in mind ", but no body keeps any thing in *ling*. On reviewing the above meanings of the word, and coming last of all to "influence", especially when we know what an

amount of occult "influence" is attributed by the
Chinese to spiritual beings, to ghosts, to *fany-shui*, as
well as to living men, we are forcibly reminded
of another word found in Mark V. 30. and elsewhere :— "*virtue* had gone out of Him ". We are
not however to take *ling* as denoting the putting
forth of *virtue (dunamis)*. It is the "power" itself.
"Influence" *(influens)* is quite a different sort of
word; it could never assume a concrete sense as
"intelligence", "power", and *ling* do. It is here,
however, where *ling* seems to mean "influence",
that it comes near to the meaning of *shan*, and it
appears that the influencing Spirit of God might
be expressed by the one term as well as by the
other. No doubt the "powers" above or the
"invisible intelligences" may be said to influence
men, or level 1 things to men. *Ling* is used in this
connection (435). But the passages where Heav-
en reveals, and *shan* influences (432, 433), are
more plain and more common. To influence *ling*
(*i.e.* intelligent beings) is also more common, than
for men to be influenced by them. Men influence
intelligent beings(436, 437, 390), and perhaps the
influence is reciprocated, but nothing is taught by
this of the primary meaning of the word *ling*.

There are other expressions like permeating
shan, or being in communication or rapport with
shan, permeating *ling*, entering into *shan*, and entering into *ling ;* which are for the most part a
little obscure. Only, we can understand entering
into the spirit of a thing (294—301), not entering
into the god.

Your ling. We have seen that "your *ling*"
means "your goodness," " your powerful influence",

or "your intelligence". I have now to remark, in order to remove all doubts about the sense of *ling* being always of the complimentary kind, that as a general thing no Chinese speaks of his own *ling*. It is only in foreign-made books that we find "my *ling*"—"my *ling* hath rejoiced." *Luke* I. 47. Will any of those who adopt this rendering produce from native literature an instance of *ngo-ling*, or of *ling-loh*? I have not found such an instance; and most probably if found the reference will be to the soul or *ling-hwun*, after death; or *ngo-ling* may be found with a negative, *ngo-puh-ling*, " I am not intelligent", a phrase quite according to propriety. I am sorry that this again is a case in which it is impossible to adduce evidence; but I throw the *onus probandi* on the other side. Meantime I can produce cases of *ngo-shan* by the score. Will the authority be produced for *ling*? I mean something more than an isolated sentence. Or will native usage still be defied?

Intelligent and foolish. **Ling** is frequently found in antithesis with words meaning foolish, or stupid (158, 223, 322, 564—567, 575, 578).

Body and spirit. **Shan** is not found, like *ling*, in antithesis with foolish, but with form (22, 37, 38, 69, 80, 92, 103, 107, 142, 194, 197, 218, 311), with body (31, 76, 77, 150, 101, 283), with parts of the body (28, 65, 118, 153, 177, 39, 58, 96, 136, 113, 144, 190), and with outward appearance (79).

Materialism. There are multitudes in China who hold that the soul of man is not a spiritual substance distinct from the body, but that it is the result of the organization of matter in the body (558). With such people, and Chu-fu-tsze is one of them, though the old words *shan*, *ling*, and *hwun-p'oh* are retained, they all tend to identity of meaning (523, 524, 527, 528, &c). They are all only what might be called a " spiritual intelligence inside the air " (524), the word "air " in this case corresponding to the word *medium* in the *undulatory theory* of light (528, 576). Whereever the phenomena of intelligence *(ling)* are recognized, as in man (558) or in an idol (576, 577), the existence of *shan*, in what we call the personal sense, as a being or essence, is denied. Those who follow the popular belief that there is a " ruling spirit " (558) in man, do not indeed distinguish its substance from " air," or primary matter, and most people do not inquire into this subject at all. But the more spiritual of thinking men define *ling* differently from the materialists. The former say, "*Ling* is the essential brightness of the spirit," that is, a quality of the spirit (559, 560). This definition agrees with what we have found to be the usage, and with various definitions of *ling* by itself as " intelligence and perspicacity " (557), "understanding" (578), "knowledge" (513), " consciousness " (575).* But the latter say " Evolution is *shan* and reversion is *kwei* (521) ; this (kind of movement) is *ling*, and also the soul " (516). Hence, with them, " soul ", " spirit ", and "intelligence " are very much the same (561).

It is for Christian Missionaries to choose between the spiritualistic and materialistic definitions. A rare, very rare, use of *ling*, intelligence, by metonymy for the soul of a living man is possible.

---

* Intelligentia est mentis acies. *Cicero.*

CHAPTER V.

FURTHER ILLUSTRATIONS.

This Chapter is interposed here in order to illustrate further the usage of *shan*.   It consists chiefly of notes made years ago, and the longer quotations are not all given in the Appendix to the present essay.

I. *The Book of Rites on the Shan of men.* " When Confucius was in Wei he took notice of people attending a funeral and exclaimed, ' What a good manner of mourning they have!   It is quite a model.   Remember it my children.'   Tsze-kung said, 'What is good in it ?'   Confucius replied, ' They went as if eager after something.   They returned as if in doubt.'   Tsze-kung again asked, ' Would it not be better to hasten home to perform the seven days' ceremonial ? '   But Confucius said again, ' Remember it my children.' "

Kung Ying-tah says, on the above passage, " The filial son mourns the parent left behind, and does not know whether his *shan* is coming back after him or not; therefore he does not feel inclined to go home and seems as if in doubt.   Tsze-kung's idea was that when the burying was done, then the *shan-ling* required to be tranquillized.   Why should they not hasten home to perform the sacrificial rites and give rest to the *shan* ?   But the mourning for the parent was the radical feeling ; and the sacrifice

of peace to the *shan* was merely ceremonial. Therefore Confucius did not admit his objection."

Confucius said, " Treating the dead as dead, is
contrary to humanity, and not to be done. Treating
the dead as alive, is contrary to knowledge, and also
not to be done. Therefore there are made for them
bamboo implements, but not complete; earthen-
ware, but without finish ; wooden articles, but without planing ; harps and organs, but not tuned; and
bells, but not hung up. These are called ' bright
implements ', importing that they (the dead) are
shan-ming " (*i.e.* that their spirits are alive and intelligent, not all dead as *kwei*, ghost, would signify
522).

Chinese Note.—" To serve the dead as if they
were alive is the strongest feeling of their children.
But the way of *shan* may be different from the way
of men. The libation immediately after death approaches to treating them as men, but the funeral
approaches to treating them as *shan*. So that, in the
whole service of the dead, everything is as it were
midway between the state of man and the state of
shan."

When the head of a house dies, according to
the *Book of Rites*, the process of laying out and
dressing the corpse is commenced in the same position the person occupied when alive, because, it is
said, the filial child cannot bear to regard the parent
as dead (that is, says Ying-tah, the child cannot
bear to treat the parent as a *shan*, and to turn his
head to the north, which is the direction of darkness
whither the ghost-*shan* goes). Afterwards by two
or three separate movements the corpse is transferred
to the place where it is to be till the funeral, and

these movements are said to denote the gradual passing of the dead to (the state of) *shan*.

Is there any more of *divinity* in this word *shan* than there is in the word " spirit " in the following : —" Rest, rest, perturbed spirit " ? Achilles sacrificed to the "soul of the miserable Patroclus," which came to him in distress, twelve young Trojans besides four of his horses and two of his dogs, at the funeral pyre. *Iliad* XXIII. 65. But, had such practices any tendency to make the word (*psuchè*) " soul," assume the meaning of " god " ?

II. *Shan in the Universe. Shan* is used, in speaking of the Universe, either personally or impersonally, in strict accordance with idiom, as each man thinks. Since this word means, in man, either an enduring essence which is more or less personal, or mere excitement, it follows that, in using the same word to express their conjectures about the Universe, the Chinese may *legitimately* use it either personally or impersonally.

Emerson uses the word spirit quite legitimately when he says, "One mode of divine teaching is the incarnation of the spirit in form—in forms like my own " *(The Oversoul).* We can scarcely say the same however of the use of " God " by this author when he affirms, "O my brothers, God exists. There is a soul at the centre of nature, and over the will of every man, so that none of us can wrong the universe " *(Spiritual Laws).* His definition of what he is pleased at times to called God is precisely the same as Chu-tsze's definition of *Shang-ti*—" Thus is the universe alive. All things are moral. That *soul,* which within us is a sentiment, outside of us is a *law*. We feel its inspirations; out there in history we can see its fatal strength. It is almighty. All nature feels its grasp. It is in the world, and the world was made by it. It is eternal but it *enacts* itself in time and place " *(Compensation)*.

There are many of our countrymen who think with Schleiermacher that it is a mere matter of taste whether we believe in a personal or an impersonal God. But we cannot take any such men into our counsels. I have not met with any missionary who holds this opinion; and I think it will be universally admitted that what is spoken of as " it." in the above quotation is strikingly different from " the Jehovah of the Bible." And, far more than that, it is different from the common usage and definitions of the word " god."

Persons who hold opinions like Emerson's can only treat the word " God " in two ways. They must either exclude it from their discourse altogether, or use it in a sense entirely different from that which is understood by the mass of mankind. This latter they may do as a matter of taste; or out of deference to popular belief, because they are afraid of seeming flatly to contradict the Sacred Books. The same thing is done with *Shang-ti* in China, whether that term should be translated by " God " or by " Jove." There is indeed one other way, not often followed in Christian countries, though Emerson follows this too, namely, to speak of " God " or " Jove " as a result of evolution. *(See Parallel 8. below)*. Mr. Watters says with perfect correctness of *Lautsze's* philosophy, " *Tao*, then, is something which existed before heaven and earth were, before Deity was, and which is, indeed, eternal " (page

36). If it was "before Deity," *a fortiori* it was before God. "Deity" is not the word we want. We want a personal God.

Ten years ago, before any of Mr. Watters' Articles on "*Lao-tsu*" had appeared, in one of which he says, "the soul of Lao-tsu may have transmigrated into Emerson", I had collected a number of parallels between that American author and Hwai-nan-tsze, who flourished a century before the Christian era, and was Tauistic. But indeed there is a great deal of the same sort in all Chinese philosophers. If the doctrine of a personal God, *versus* an impersonal, is to be settled by a majority of votes, the philosophers of China I fear will turn the scale against us. But what I wish to observe is, that the use of "spirit" (or "mind") by Emerson corresponds exactly to the use of *shan* by the same class of thinkers in China ; and that both usages are perfectly idiomatic. We recognize in both words the same amount of vagueness, not put into the words by these writers, but found in them. The vagueness belongs to the words as a part of their nature. I give only a few examples ; the parallelism might be carried out to any extent.

Parallel 1.

" The universe is one man's body, all it contains is one man's work. Therefore heaven and earth cannot frighten him who understands nature, miracles cannot deceive him who can judge of the fitness of things. Hence the sage gets a knowledge of distant things from things near, and all varieties become unity. The men of remote antiquity united their *shan* with heaven and earth (the universe), and were free men of their age."

·   *Hwai-nan-tsze* § VIII.

"There is one mind common to all individual men. Every man is an inlet to the same and to all of the same. He that is once admitted to the right of reason is made a free man of the whole estate. What Plato has thought he may think, what a saint has felt he may feel, what at any time has befallen any man he can understand. Who has access to this universal mind, is a party to all that is or can be done, for this is the only and sovereign agent."

Emerson—History.

Parallel 2.

"The mind is the lord of the body, and *shan* is the mind's precious thing."

Hwai-nan-tsze § VII.

"Nothing is at last sacred but the integrity of our own minds."

Emerson—Self Reliance.

Parallel 3.

"If you cannot restrain yourself, then give way. If you give way your *shan* will not resent it."

Hwai-nan-tsze § XII.

"Accept your genius, and say what you think."

Emerson—Spiritual Laws.

Parallel 4.

"The purer essence of the mind may by its *shan* influence men, though it may not be able to teach them."

Hwai-nan-tsze § X.

" Who has more soul than I masters me though he should not raise his finger. Round him I must revolve by the gravitation of spirits. Who has less, I rule with like facility.

Emerson—Self-Reliance.

Parallel 5.

" He whom demons will not dare to vex, and on whom the *shan* of mountains and streams will not dare to send calamities, is most noble " (the nobility of perfect virtue).

Hwai-nan-tsze § IX.

" All the devils respect virtue."

Emerson—Spiritual Laws.

Parallel 6.

" To enter into the mystic sympathy and perfect blending of *shan*, and to roam in the place where hands and hearts are all emptiness—where there is no connection with material things, is what a father cannot teach his son. The musician's art by which he expresses ideas, imitates things, and images *shan*, as his fingers dance over the chords, is what a brother cannot impart to a brother " (See 287).

Hwai-nan-tsze § IX.

" Why insist on rash personal relations with your friend ? * * Leave this touching and clawing. Let him be to me a spirit " (210).

Emerson—Friendship.

" One class live to the utility of the symbol ; esteeming health and wealth a final good. Another class live above this mark to the beauty of the symbol, as the poet, and artist, and the naturalists, and the man of science. A third class live above the beauty of the symbol to the beauty of the thing signified; these are wise men. The first class have common sense, the second taste, and the third spiritual perception."

Ibid—Prudence.

Parallel 7.

" The universal mind is diffused through everything. Man gets it, and it is man's mind. Other creatures get it, and it is their mind. Trees and plants, birds and beasts communicate with it, and it is the mind of trees and plants, birds and beasts. It is all one universal mind."

Chu-tsze—On Heaven and Earth.

" All creatures partake of the (impalpable) ether of the whole. Man has it correct and complete, so he stands with his head erect. Beasts have it in a partial manner, and so their heads are in a horizontal position. Plants again have their heads in the ground and their tails straight above."

Ibid.

" These appearances indicate the fact that the universe is represented in every one of its particles. Everything in nature contains all the powers of nature. Everything is made of one hidden stuff, as the naturalist sees one type under every metamorphosis, and regards a horse as a running man, a fish as a swimming man, a bird as a flying man, a tree as a rooted man."

Emerson—Compensation.

Parallel 8.

" *Tau* " (an abstraction) " seems to have been before *Ti* " *(Shang-ti).*

Lau-tsze (486).

" *Tau* gives spiritual existence to demons and *Ti's*" *(Shang-ti's)*.   *Chwang-tsze* (484).

" One ever-present *ling*."*
Note on Chwang-tsze (485).

" The mind has its motion and its rest. In itself it is called (the power of) Change (alternation 易). Its Law is called Reason. Its *operation* is called *shan*."
Chu-tsze—On Mind.

" *Shan* is the *operation* of *Ti* " *(Shang-ti)*.
Yik-king, Comm. (488).

" The Universe has three *children, born* at one *time,* which re-appear under different names, in every system of thought, whether they be called cause, *operation,* and effect; or more poetically Jove, Pluto, Neptune; or theologically, the Father, the *Spirit*†, and the Son; but which we call here the Knower, the Doer, and the Sayer."
Emerson—The Poet.

Parallel 9.

" Therefore the ghost-*shan* of my own *shan*, of my object of worship, and of the system of nature, are all one and the same."
Notes on the Doctrine of the Mean.

" The superior man performs worship all in and for himself; therefore the highest worship is spiritual (*shan*). The highest worship is spiritual (*shan*) and the vulgar make it double " (suppose a distinction between subject and object), " therefore they cannot attain to it."
Han-Fei-tsze § XX.

---

*This expression reminds us of *Nous*, but it is not Chwang-tsze's own.
†Observe " operation " takes the place of " spirit " and of *shan*.

"Ineffable is the union of man and God in
every act of the soul. The simplest person, who
in his integrity worships God, becomes God; yet
forever and ever the influx of this better and universal self is new and unsearchable ; ever it inspires
awe and astonishment.

Emerson—The Over-soul.

Nothing can be more obvious than that the
word *shan* in the above Chinese examples corresponds to the " soul," "mind," " spirit " and "over-
soul " in Emerson's writings—not to "God" which
he brings in occasionally by a kind of poetical
license, or as a metaphor borrowed from the language of theology.

Parallel 10.

" There are 10,000 *shan* in the human body.
If a man receives spiritual essence and nourishes
his body, inhales air and refines his form ; then
the 10,000 *shan* will each hold its true place. But
if not, the glorious garrison will fade away—the
10,000 *shan* will die."

Biography of Genii—Pang-tsu (417).

" The 10,000 *shan* are one *shan*."

Ts'i-k'iu-tsze (389).

Tauist Books speak of the " The *shan* of
the eyes, of the nose, of the month, of the
tongue, of the teeth, &c., &c. The *shan* of the
human body are so many, it is impossible to count
them." " The 84,000 individual downy hairs all
turn into protecting *shan*, but one *shan* in the
heart rules them all."

Hwang-t'ing-king Kiai (416).

"Every line we can draw in the sand has expression; and there is no body without its spirit or
genius."

Emerson—The Poet.

III. *Poetical and figurative uses of shan.* The
last quotation brings us near to a branch of the subject on which it is needless to dwell, further than to
call attention to the wonderful agreement between
shan and "spirit or genius." An artist first attains
to expression with his pencil, and then he gets, by
another stage, the very *shan* of it (290). The *shan*
of a person is communicated to his portrait by an
artist (243 292). The same is done in drawing a
picture of a bamboo or any object in nature (291).
Chwang-tsze puts into his writings the *shan* of Lau-
tsze (292). Music can express the *shan* (293).
When a person imitates another's performances to
the life it is called a "*shan* resemblance" (310).
A poet describes the *shan* of hope (307), or "the
shan of smiting upon his breast and winging his
hands" (grief or despair 548). A man whose fea-
tures are not like another's, but whose expression or
manner occasionally remind you forcibly of the other,
is like him in *shan* (311). An artist who has attained
to the mystery of his art is *shan-miau*, spiritually
mysterious, *i.e.* has a genius inscrutable to others
(309). And his peculiar faculty or genius *(shan)*
cannot be imparted to any. It is like the faculty
or genius (*shan*) of the eye for seeing which cannot
be communicated to the ear or to any other organ of
the body (287). A magical doctor could see the
shan of a disease, before there were any symtoms,
and remove it (319*a*).

CHAPTER VI.

THIRD SENSE OF SPIRIT—*LING, SHAN*, AND *TI*.

When it is said, "The *shan* of Heaven settles in the sun, as the *shan* (spirit) of man settles in the eye", the parallelism leaves it impossible to suppose any metonymy in the case. So also, when we read in the *Book of Poetry* (III. iii. 5), " The great mountains sent down *shan*" (430), taking the native commentary, and not the translation, as our guide, we understand that these mountains sent down "their spiritual influence and harmonious air", or else "the harmonious air of their spiritual intelligence". In short the *ling* of the mountains, in the sense in which many missionaries use the word, "their spirits, descended." Again, when in the *Confucian Analects*, "the T'ai Mountain is said to be " discerning" (III. 6), or "the mountains and rivers" capable of discerning the colour of "a calf" to be offered to them in sacrifice (VI. 4), and the commentators tell us that " the *shan* of these mountains and rivers " are referred to ; we can understand that *shan* is the same as "spirit " or "soul." This usage is very common. All beings, from *Shang-ti* down to the smallest material object that the eye can see (a hair for example 415, 416), have spirits *(shan)*. But now we come to another usage of this word, the usage about which all the controversy is. Heaven itself, those mountains and rivers themselves, men, beasts, birds, fishes, insects, stones, and, most common of all, graven images themselves are called *shan.* It is about the first and last of these, Heaven and graven images, that practically our inquiry is concerned. The objects of worship of the Chinese generally speaking are Heaven, Heaven and Earth, their ancestors, and images, made mostly in the form of men and women. They do indeed habitually burn insense and make bows and gesticulations in the open air and into the void ; but the objects then are so vague, that, though called *shan*, or *kwei-shan*, or *kwei*, they scarcely come under the class of beings which we call " the gods." As a rule an object of worship of any note or definiteness has an image and a temple. This then is what we call " a god" or " an idol", and the Chinese call it a *shan.* And the contention of those whom I, with all the earnestness of which I am capable, seek to lead into another way of thinking, is that, since the Chinese speak habitually of Heaven and Earth, their ancestors, and their idols as *shan*, the first great object of the Christian missionary ought to be, to convince them that the entire usage of this word from the earliest dawn of their history down to the present time, in all its diversities of application and in all its ramifications in their literature, is founded on ignorance, error, and sin ; that the word properly means " god"; and that having never known the true God they have never used this word in its true and proper sense. In short all *shan* hitherto known in China, according to this view, are " false *shan*," while the word, as an adjective, means divine ; and, as an

impersonal noun, deity or divinity. They do not
state their argument precisely as I have done;
but their translations of the Scriptures and daily
accumulating volumes of Hymns, Discourses,
Tracts, &c. are my authority for saying, they want
to throw this word out of the Chinese language in
every sense except that of God, gods, and divine.
Even *tsing-shan* cannot be used in such a place as
Judges XV. 19, "his spirit came again and he
revived", but the "spirit" has to be expressed by
tsing-k'i, "subtile breath." And all this follows
quite naturally; for the Christian religion and
theology cannot be taught with a word for God
which may, at the same time, be correctly used
for the human soul, or spirit.

Spiritual and intelligent men. *Shan* is used
by metonymy for "spiritual men" (324, 326, 327);
ling is used by metonymy for "intelligent men"
(320, 321, 322, 325, 340); and *Ti* is used by
metonymy for the Emperor of China, the vice-
gerent of Heaven. The last statement will be
discussed in next chapter. The other two will
probably not be disputed. *Shan* is used where we
should say "genius." in the personal sense. One
man is a "flower-genius" because he excels in the
cultivation of flowers (328); another is a "tea-
genius" because he wrote three volumes on tea
(329), a third is a "genius of strong drink" because of his extraordinary capacity for it (330).
These are metaphoric uses of *shan* which decide
nothing as to its being "god" or "spirit."

Spiritual and intelligent things. To this class
I refer the grosser kind of things which are so de-
signated. To the vulgar mind aerial beings are

pure spirits. _Of course it is only a question of de-gree, where there is no recognition of spirit as an essence entirely distinct from matter. Let us not shrink from the fact. Every body, be he Jew or Gentile, who has not clearly made up his mind, that "a spirit" is a being independent of matter and distinct from it, so that he would be a complete per-sonal being if all that is called matter (air, ether, and imponderable *media* included) were annihilated, must think of God himself as in some respect mate-rial. That many excellent and pious men have done so, is, I think, easily ascertained. The confounding of air with spirit has been all but universal among mankind; e.s. *tsing-k'i* above. The present-para-graph has nothing to do with "trifles light as air." Things of the grosser kind seem to be more frequently called *ling* than *shan*. I can only explain this on the ground that, *ling* being merely a quality, the metonymy is more obvious than in the case of *shan*, which may denote an etherial substance, without any figure of speech. Hence to speak of mankind in general as *shan* would cause confusion of ideas and suggest something of an etherial nature perhaps belonging to our bodies; whereas *shang-ling*, "liv-ing intelligences," is a common designation of men (320). Hence also the firmament is called "the round intelligence" (343) the nine heavens, "the nine intelligences" (344); the moon "the shady in-telligence" (345). A gigantic being who tore as-sunder with his hands the heavens and the earth at the command of *Shang-ti* is called the "big intelli-gence" (346). Heaven, Earth, and Man are called " the three *ling*", or " the three *shun*" (350). The sun, moon, and stars are also " three *ling*" (349)

The four *ling* are the unicorn, phœnix, tortoise, and dragon (351). The five *ling* are five creatures of different colours representing the five elements (352). Then, long before there were *shan* of clay and wood (idols 356), there were "grass-*ling*" (354), a sort of rude figures anciently used at funerals. And, not only is the soul of the dead called *ling*, but the material things, in or near which the soul is supposed to hover, are included in this name (355). In all these cases the metonymy is evident. It is not so clear however when it is said that a Tauist's bones, that do not decay, are *shan* (spirit 357). It seems as if the bones might "turn all to spirit", as the angel told Adam he might do, in *Paradise Lost*.

Here I must again give a few parallel passages to illustrate the more concrete use of *shan*.

Parallel 1.

"That which, when it would be small, becomes like a moth or a grub, when it would be large, fills the world; when it would ascend, mounts on the airy clouds, when it would descend, enters the deep; whose transformations are not conditioned by days, nor its ascending or descending by seasons, is called *shan* (496). *Kwan-tsze.**

        "For spirits when they please
"Can either sex assume, or both; so soft
"And uncompounded is their essence pure,
"Not ty'd or manackled with joint or limb,
"Nor founded on the brittle strength of bones,
"Like cumbrous flesh; but in what shape they
    choose,

---

* 管子.

" Dilated or condensed, bright or obscure,
" Can execute their airy purposes,
" And works of love or enmity fulfil."

Paradise Lost I.

Parallel 2.

" No *shan* is left uninvoked."

Book of Poetry.

The spirit of draught is described as a man
three feet high, naked, and having his eyes in the
crown of his head. All sorts were propitiated in
time of distress (448, 457).

"O all ye host of heaven ! O earth ! What
else ? And shall I couple hell ?   *Hamlet.*

Parallel 3.

" When Hwan prince of Ts'e (B.C. 685—642)
was on an expedition against the north, at Ku-chuh,
he saw a man of a foot high, with clothes, cap, and
ornamental cuffs, running before his horses. Kwan-
chung said, ' This is the *shan* of the mountain. Its
name is *Yü-'rh*. When a usurping prince arises it
appears.' "   *Shuh-i-ki.*

"Dr. Percy tells us that the existence of fairies
is alluded to by the most ancient British bards, among
whom the commonest name was that of 'spirits of
the mountains.' "   *Brand's Popular Antiquities.*

Parallel 4.

" The carp, as soon as its scales number 360, is
caught and carried away by dragons ; but if every
year a *shan* be placed to guard it, it cannot be carried away. *This shan* is a tortoise " (358).

Shuh-i-ki.

"A spirit called the *hairy one*, in the Isle of Man, cut down and gathered in the meadow-grass which would have been injured if allowed to remain exposed to the coming storm." *Brand.*

Instances like the above could be multiplied to any extent. There is not a fairy or ghost story in our language, but might be matched with a Chinese one in which the subject is *shan*.

Things that are gods. Some one has quoted the passage in which it is said certain people's "god is their belly," as showing the extensive *generic* use of "god" *(theos)*. Here is a parallel case of *ti*, used figuratively:—" In a dry year, the earth-dragon ; and in pestilence, the grass-dog (figures made to remove the evils) are *ti* (gods) for the time being " (359).

Worshipped beings. I have quoted passages to show that *ti*, *shan*, and *ling* in many combinations referring to objects of worship are synonymous or nearly so. The Supreme *Ti*, the Supreme *Shan*, and the Supreme *Ling*, all mean, or may mean, the God of Heaven (360—366). Let none of my brethren be alarmed or offended, as if I meant to say that the Chinese know a great deal about the God of Heaven, which they are supposed *a priori* not to know till we tell them. I wish to affirm nothing as to the amount of their knowledge; and no man can be more deeply convinced than I am of their need of teaching. But these terms, in some connections, all mean the Most High. *Chi-shan* means the same in the passage quoted (367), though it is rather pantheistic. The next following expressions, referring to the firmament, are of a somewhat material nature (368—372). It must also be noticed that *shan* and *ling* have a strong tendency to be plural and to include too much, especially *shan* (363)—"the spirits of the souls that are above." Observe also the difference between *shan* and *ling* in the explanation of "high intelligences", namely, "the spirits of heaven that have intelligence", as if some might be without that quality *(ling)*. All three words are used in the plural with equal freedom. I should say, the four terms, *shang-ti, ti, shan,* and *ling* have all more or less of a plural use. There is no question about the last two, and not so much about the second, But the first, *shang-ti*, has also decidedly a plural use. In the *Chow Ritual,* *shang-ti* alone is generic (378), and an epithet has to be added to distinguish the Highest One. With the Tauists "all the *shang-ti* of heaven" are thirty-two or thirty-six (381, 382). This is not a mere poetic license, as "the thirty-six *yuh-hwang*" (384) appears to be. The use is fully established in Tauist Books (388). There are also not a few *shang-ti* whose names are well known (383). Then, if we want a word with a still wider scope, we have "ten thousand *ti*" (388), and "the host of *ti*" (392), by only dropping the *shang*. Is this not generic enough? On the other hand, there is *ling* also quite as comprehensive as *shan* itself for objects of worship, not indeed in such common use, but still usable. It is my serious conviction that to adopt *ling* for objects of worship would be less injurious than to adopt *shan*, because the former is not nearly of such frequent occurrence in other senses nor so varied in its uses as the latter. But it is not practicable to adopt either. Again, in Canton and other places, it is well known that *pu-sah* is quite as commonly used for objects of worship as *shan*, and *pu-sah* has the great advantage of being confined very much to that sense. Is not common usage for objects of worship utterly inadequate to prove a word equivalent to "god or gods"? Our word "idol" would denote very much all the objects of worship of the Chinese people of the present day; but we know well "idol" is not the same sort of word as "God." Neither is "spirit" the same sort of word. If there ever really was a race of Red Indians who worshipped "the Great Spirit," it would have been necessary probably for missionaries to substitute some other term for "Spirit", as Great One or Great Being, in order to relieve this word for its proper use in the Christian theology. This is at all events the case with *shan;* whatever strong reasons any one may see for using it for "God" and "gods", in translating the Bible and teaching Christianity, there are far stronger for retaining it for "spirit"; because, to use a familiar phrase, there will be a dead lock, if the right native word is not available for spirit.

Evil spirits and possession. As, at the outset of our investigation, we found *shan* alone good for the spirit of a living man, so now, at the close, we take leave of all other terms but this. There are no evil *ling*, unclean *ling*, or possessions by *ling*, in my collection. If I had found such I would have put them in. Will my Christian brethren trust me thus far? Then, as for *shan*, look at the passages quoted, and, if they are insufficient, I will bring double the number on a few days warning. There are evil *shan*, malignant *shan*, wicked *shan*, lewd *shan*, fierce *shan*, scorching *shan*, pesti-

lential *shan*, and unclean *shan* (442—453). There
are *shan* whom people run against innocently and
unawares, and who thereupon inflict upon them
every kind of misery (453, 454). Sin is laid to the
charge of *shan*(455), attempts are made to slay them
(456), and, failing that, offerings and religious service are rendered to them, when of course oppro-
brious names will be dropt, and flattering titles
given to them, but all along they were called *shan*
(457, 458). *Shan* come sometimes on invitation
and take possession of men's bodies, when they
lose for a time their personal identity, and the *shan*
act and speak, eat and drink through them, and
even get intoxicated, as we read in the *Book of
Poetry*, the oldest book in China; the phenomena
there recorded being precisely the same in nature as
modern possession by demons (460). The evil *shan*
at other times come uninvited, without any assign-
able cause, and torment people (451). A man
when under the power of such *shan* is called a
wizard, and a woman in the same condition is called
a witch (462). Possession by *ling* is something new
in Chinese. A "familiar spirit" may be a *kwei*, or
a *shan*, but not a *ling*.

CHAPTER VII.

HEAVEN, *TI*, AND *SHANG-TI*.

There are a great many Chinese quotations in the Appendix which have been touched on but lightly, or not at all. They are put on record as bearing on the subject, for future use, in the belief that they may be helpful towards the final settlement of the question. I am not aware of having overlooked any passage which tells on the opposite side; and I should like to see some quotations from Chinese authors to prove, for instance, that *ling* is used for the human spirit; or that "my *shan*" is usable for "my God", or that *Ti* is any thing different from what I have represented that word to be. If such passages were before me now, I should be delighted to put them in where they ought to go, so as to complete the evidence on both sides. I might here wind up with the remark, that *Shang-ti* for "God" needs no words of recommendation from me. It is the word we find in the language for the Highest. It is not indeed the Jehovah of the Jews, nor the Theos of the Greeks, nor the God of English Christians; and, at the same time, it is not the Jove of the Romans, or the Baal of the Canaanites, or the Great Spirit of the Red Indians; but it is the word corresponding to God in Chinese as near as we could wish or expect. Take it and be thankful; or, if not, find another, the use of which will not render co-operation impracticable, and conference on mission work a mere name for nothing. ' It must be apparent to any sensible man, without a knowledge of Chinese, that between those who freely use the word *shan* in all the senses described in this essay, and those who say, " there is none *shan* but one, that is, God ", there can be no effective co-operation or consultation about their work. We divide at the very threshold, we contradict each other in every sermon or prayer or hymn we make; our versions of the Scriptures read like two different Books; the disregard of idiom, in the case before us, is followed up by a general disregard of idiom, and a dislike of what is deemed undue pandering to Chinese taste on the other side. Then, the other side are driven to the Classics and standard literature for confirmation of their usage; and, finding indeed what they want, they are liable to be too much fascinated by ornaments of style, and thus they are impeded in their usefulness, as well as laid open to the charge brought against them. What a waste of power this question has caused and is causing, God knows; and we are all in our measure responsible for it to Him.

Objections answered. 1. *Shang-ti* is, in the usage of the Confucianists, too much like the visible heavens personified. 2. *Shang-ti* is, by the Tauists, and by the people generally, applied to various idols, here to *Yuh-hwang*, there to *Huen-tien*, and again to *Kwan-kung*, to one, or two, or more indeed, but not to the whole pantheon. 3. *Shang-ti* contains in it the idea of supremacy. 4. *Shang-ti* cannot be used naturally and properly in the plural. 5. By using this term we seem to be taking the chief god of the Confucianists, or the chief god of the Tauists, to be our God. 6. The second syllable of the term is equivalent to Emperor, and denotes in fact the Emperor of China.—That these objections are founded on facts no one can deny. I object to some of the facts, that is to say, I wish that they were not facts; but their validity as objections to the term is far from apparent. Let me illustrate this by means of the first objection and the second. The Confucianists were long before the Tauists in their use of this word. Lau-tsze, the founder of the Tauist system, knew nothing about those idols referred to, and probably no one would have been more horrified than himself at the idea of giving such a name to such things. Confucius, on the other hand, who lived about the same time (B.C. 551—478), did not initiate the practice of calling Heaven personified *Shang-ti*. The usage came down with the language from unfathomable antiquity. " Heaven " and *Ti* and *Shang-ti* were used almost synonymously, in the old *Ballads** which he recited, and which he cherished as perhaps the most precious heritage of antiquity. Grant then for the moment that *Shang-ti* is Heaven, even if it does not coincide with our theological conception, are not the Tauists just as much in error as if it did? And shall we not join the Confucianists in a holy alliance against the blasphemy of calling an image of clay Heaven? In my humble opinion we might do many worse things; as for instance, we might occupy ourselves in adducing far-fetched arguments against each other, which would be a much more questionable thing than taking the Confucianists' word for God, even it be in

---

* See *Note* B.

their mouths a little like Jove.* I can with great good reason object to the Tauist usage of *Shang-ti*; a course which no one is justified in adopting in regard to the universal usage of *shan* for spirits whether objects of worship or not. The objections brought against *Shang-ti* are, as far as I can ascertain them, either objectionable things, or else really recommendations to the word. The definiteness, the strong personality of the term, and the fact that it denotes the chief gods of *two* existing sects, and not of one only, are really recommendations. We can come in between them, and say, "You are both in a measure wrong. That Being, whom one of you ignorantly makes to be Heaven personified, or the animated Cosmos, and the other still more ignorantly makes to be an image of clay, or the king of Fairy-Land, and at the same time also the god of the North Pole, that Being, whose sacred name you have both profaned by giving it to men, as to *Kwan-kung*, and in one of its forms to your emperor,—Him declare we unto you. Not only certain of your own poets, but the universal consent of your wisest men, we can adduce, to shew, that this name, whether *Ti* or *Shang-ti*, means properly Heaven, or 'the Lord of Heaven', and nothing else. Do not tell us that *Shang-ti* is the proper name of an idol. It is the most improper of all names that could be named. We tell you, the Almighty has revealed himself, and He has given an authoritative command, saying, 'Thou shalt have no other *shang-ti* before me.' " The word *is* used in the plural. This also is an established usage of the

---

* The name of the Supreme Deity among the Romans. *Webster*.

Chinese language, and it is obviously an improper
usage. But can any one show a good reason for
refusing the word because of the *obviousness* of this
impropriety? If there were really no impropriety
in saying "gods", then the plural form would be
in accordance with the truth of things. Should
we not rejoice to find a word for God in Chinese,
like *Shang-ti*, of which the impropriety of a plural
use is rather more apparent; considering that the
language has no inflections; and that "to worship
God" and "to worship the gods", while we use
the same name throughout, are not distinguishable
from one another? Just consider it one moment.
The Chinese will very soon find out that we do
not worshp *Huen-tien*, or *Yuh-hwang*, or the Emperor, or the visible Heavens. We are liable to
be mistaken by very ignorant people and perfect
strangers in this way, and we are liable to be teased
also by impertinent questioners who know better.
But that we do not worship certain visible and
very substantial things may soon be known. That
is not the difficulty. The difficulty is to let them
know what we really do worship; and, to all but
the initiated, "worship *shan*", in the light of the ex-
position here given of the meanings of *shan*, must
convey a very vague notion indeed. We must
ever remember that what we do now, we do, not
merely for those at present under our instruction
or those to whom we give a Bible or a Tract, but
for a great nation and a long future; and the liabil-
ity of mistaking *Shang-ti* for *Yuh-hwang* is of a
temporary, local, and trivial nature, while the
teaching of spirit-worship is a radical mistake as
to theology, and a deviation from what we are sent

here to teach, which may result in very serious consequences. The mistake is of an inward and spiritual kind, and so are the consequences—not easily estimated.

Lord of Heaven (379). The term *T'ien-chu* is just one of the Chinese definitions of *Ti* and *Shang-ti* (469, 470, 478, 480). There are many other definitions of *Ti*, e. g. " *Ti* is Heaven " (463, 464, 466, 467). " *Ti* is the Spirit of Heaven" (465), " *Ti* is the heart or mind of Heaven " (467, 468). "*Ti* is the Nature of Heaven " (471). "*Ti* is Law" (472, 473). " There is not a *Shang-ti* like the images men make " (474, 480). " There is not a Man (Person) in Heaven who issues decrees as the old books *seem* to say (473); nevertheless, in reading those old books, it seems impossible to exclude altogether the notion of something more than Law, and in order to realize what they mean by the decrees of *Shang-ti*, or Heaven, we must " (in the private opinion of the speaker, Chu-tsze) " include the idea of the visible Heaven as that which decrees " (479). In spite of this materialistic tendency of the philosophical interpreters, they had long ago made up their minds that "the visible Heaven and *Shang-ti* must be distinct," and that "*Shang-ti* has no bodily form " (465—468, 479, 480). The questionings of thoughtful men, of a sceptical nature, which have come down from before the Christian era (475, 476), are deserving of our earnest attention. Compare the two passages here referred to with the xxxviiith chapter of Job beginning at the 5th verse—" Who hath laid the measures thereof?" Then look at the unsatisfactory conclusion of the second questioner, Chwang-tsze;—"It seems as if there were a True

Ruler, only we cannot get at His *personality*" (477).
Chwang-tsze does not make use of the personal name
(Shang-ti) here, or elsewhere as a rule, just because
he could not "get hold of the personality" of the
Deity. And Chu-tsze admires his unanswered questions, saying, "Chwang-tsze perceived this principle;
the (Ruler or) Ruling Power is self-existent, inher-
ent, necessary, unspeakable. You must see it for
yourself" (478). I give only the sense of the original. "Self-existent" with Chu-tsze does not here
refer to a Being but to a Law which Heaven has in
itself.

The above are a few of the answers the Chinese
have attempted to give to the question, "What is
God?" We find among them "God is the Spirit
of Heaven," and "God is the Ruler or Lord of
Heaven." Can there be any hesitancy about pre-
ferring the plastic word itself *(Ti* or *Shang-ti)* to the
one rigid definition of it *(T'ien-chu)*, "Lord of
Heaven?"

Ruler. Perfect precision of language is not
attainable; and often, when aiming at precision in
one direction, we err egregiously, without perceiving
it, in another. Apart from all abstruse discussions
about the nature of God, the two words "lord"
(chu) and "ruler" *(tsai)* are equally concrete and
personal, and amount very much to the same thing.
To make the two together, *chu-tsai*, equivalent to
"Ruling Power" is a device of pantheistic or atheistic
philosophy. But observe what has been done, on
our own part, in this debate about Terms for God.
One Chinese definition, of *Ti* and *Shang-ti* alike,
has been taken and translated into English as "the
Ruler of Heaven," then cut in two, and the least

significant part of it retained for use—"Ruler," "ruler." Following upon this we have an interminable logomachy. On the one hand, there is an elaborate argument to shew that "God" also has the relative sense of "Ruler"; whilst, on the other, this is denied, and a beautiful *argumentum ad hominem* appears, to the effect that "ruler" is utterly inadequate to express "God." All this is just like taking out one of Webster's definitions, "the Sovereign of the Universe", dropping the latter part of it, and, then seeking, from the uses and meanings of "Sovereign," to determine the nature of the word "God." Sovereign is a relative term, and so also is Lord. But, nevertheless, does not common sense suggest, since the Romanists have chosen this very phrase "the Lord of Heaven", in Chinese, for "God", and not a few Protestants and Anglicans are inclined to follow their example, that the native phrase, *t'ien-chi-chu-tsai*, "the Lord and Ruler of Heaven," when taken *entire*, is one of the best definitions of God which can be given? Else, why should the definition be preferred to the very word itself? Can there be any satisfaction to an ingenuous mind in the maintenance of such a discussion as this about "Ruler" or "ruler"? If any one lays hold of any inadvertence or want of precision in my language, and founds a similar argument upon it against the truth, I can only answer him with silence. *Ti* is nòt "ruler", but "Ruler of Heaven."

Emperor. The modern use of this word or its equivalent, "Imperator," dates from the time of Julius Cæsar. The use of *Hwang-ti* and *Ti*, for the Sovereign of China, dates from Ts'in Shi, about two centuries earlier. But, the origin of the two titles, the Roman and the Chinese, and their primary meanings are quite as different as the two men just named were different the one from the other. Julius Cæsar *was* an *imperator*. Ts'in Shi was not a *ti* (either Heaven or God) although he impiously called himself this. This act of Ts'in Shi may be made intelligible to all readers by transferring the account of it given by Sze-ma Ts'ien, in a figure, to Julius Cæsar. Suppose that Cæsar, in the height of his power, had called together the Roman Senate, to consult about what title he should assume. The Senators, with fear and trembling, suggest that, according to the veritable traditions of Rome, one of the early kings was styled " Superbus Rex," and that Cæsar might assume that honorable title. But Cæsar here interposes and says, " Put away the ' Rex,' and retain the ' Superbus.' Then, make a further selection from the veritable traditions you speak of. Was not the founder of Rome called ' Deus Deo natus '? Call me therefore '*Superbus Deus*' " (334). There is not a single point exaggerated in this imaginary illustration. The traditions of China were three or four fold more remote, and fully as incredible, as those of Rome which were put on record as veritable history by Livy. And the credulity of some European scholars who to this day accept without question the statement of the Chinese *Book of History*, that the first two sovereigns of China, who reigned 2,000 years before Ts'in Shi, were " *Ti* "; while, during the intervening period of two millenniums, no human being was so entitled, and the name *Ti* belonged to Heaven alone, is a mystery I cannot fathom.* But I venture here to throw out one mild suggestion, which may lead to profitable reflection. "Emperor" is a western word, very special in its application, and, as far as I know, never applied to God. It so happens that this word suits our purposes in translation, where *ti* and *hwang-ti* denote the sovereign of China. But where is our logic, if, after translating the Chinese title in this way, we reason back from our own translation to the meaning of *Ti*? Would it subserve the interests of truth to construct another beautiful *argumentum ad hominem* founded on Dr. Legge's translation of the *Book of History*, Part I. and Part II., referring to the two sovereigns aforesaid as *(ti)* "emperors" far back in "antiquity"? Is the translation inspired? It would be well to read the Translator's *Notes*, in this connection, where the uniform testimony of natives is given, that "*Ti* means Heaven," that those two men were called *ti* because their virtue was equal to Heaven, and that the sovereigns of China have been, since Ts'in Shi, called by the same title "as the vicegerents of Heaven" *i.e.* by metonymy. Before Ts'in Shi the sovereigns of China had been called "celestial kings" *(t'ien-wang)*, but, since his time, the noun (Cœlus or Deus) has taken the place of the adjective; yea, even the name of "the Lord and Ruler of Heaven" has been freely given to them. But it should be remembered that the same title is not freely given to any other earthly potentate, or ruler. If the Chinese could have their will, we should not only be still called "barbarians," but our sovereigns would receive, instead of

---

° See *Notes* A and B. It might have been said of Ts'in Shi, as it was said of Domitian, "Dominum se et Deum primus appellari jussit." *Eutropius.*

hwang-ti, the humbler title of "sons of heaven" *(t'ien-tsze)* to intimate their inferiority (464).   We laugh at " the Celestials "; but nevertheless we demand, in our intercourse with them, that a title equivalent to " the God of Heaven " shall be given to our kings.

In conclusion, as I said of *shan* so I say of *ti,* no metaphoric use of the word can alter its radical meaning; and much less can the abuse of it have this effect.   An extensive and impartial examination of the usages of a word seems to me the only legitimate means of ascertaining what its radical meaning, and metaphoric uses or abuses are.   My aim has been to find and set forth the truth, the whole truth, and nothing but the truth, in regard to those three terms, *shan, ling,* and *ti.*   If I have failed in any particular it will probably be found to have arisen from taking too narrow a range, and possessing too superficial a knowledge of the Chinese language.   Of one thing I am convinced, that a less comprehensive view of the language, and the introduction of more ancient western lore, will only promote darkness and confusion.   If I am ever to get new light on this subject, or if any one else is going to place it in a new and better light, it must be by following out the same line of investigation here pursued more perfectly, and, I can add with a clear conscience, in the same spirit.

Note A, Historical.

Imagine yourself in China in the time of Confucius (B C. 551 — 478) instead of in the ninteenth century. Very different was China then. It was indeed a very old nation, having more than a millennium of history, some say 18 centuries, but very dark in the early parts (341).

1. There were as yet. it appears, no idols in China.

2. In the *Old Ballad Book;* the only book which Confucius required his pupils to master, "Heaven," *Ti*, and *Shang-ti* were used almost synonymously, and the other objects of worship, parts of nature, and souls of men, were spoken of generally as *poh-shan* (hundred spirits).

3. No emperor of China was as yet called *Ti*. If there ever was a quibble, the quoting of a satyrical Ode (II. vii. X.) against this is one. "This *Shang-ti* is very *shan*" refers to the emperor, but neither *Shang-ti* nor *shan* is his title. So also a charming lady is compared both to Heaven and to *Ti* (I. iv. III). We have all read what the Indian poet styled the Prince of Wales

4 Confucius could not give a credible account of the two dynasties preceding his own for want of documents. There must have been very few Books.

5. But, men then strove hard to make the *Book of History* extend back even beyond these dynasties ; and Confucius himself, falling in with the popular craving for a grand origin, imagined he saw far back in antiquity two divine men, whose virtue corresponded to Heaven.

6. In the *Confucian Analects*, even these two are not spoken of as *Ti;* and, considering that Mencius, two centuries later, pronounced the *Book of History* as he had it incredible in many parts, we may suppose that what we have now is by no means the same that was approved by Confucius; and thus we may acquit him of the charge of styling a human being *Ti* or Heaven.

7. Since the History of those 18 centuries, as we have it now, opens with two *Ti*, and there are no other beings, but Heaven and these two, counted worthy of such a title, we must conclude that these two were deified, if not by Confucius, then by the writer of the first two parts of the *History*, and by Mencius.

8. The authoritative publication of the first commandment in the form "Thou shalt have no other *Ti* besides me," would have had a powerful significance at that time, when the notion was growing up that the first sovereigns of the Empire were *Ti*.

9. Many sayings were in after ages imputed to Confucius which in all probability he never uttered. It was said, for example, that he was well aware of the existence of "five *Ti*," who reigned

in succession in ancient China; and, further still, of "three August Ones" who reigned before the "five *Ti*."

10.   In uncritical ages, mankind easily believed such inventions. But, strangest of all is the last discovery, that Confucius was well acquainted with a person of the name of *P'an-ku*,* who lived and reigned ages before the three and the five; the fact being that, historically, P'an-ku was the invention of a dreamy Tauist† in his dotage, on the top of Lo-fau-shan in Kwang-tung, a good thousand miles away from the home of Confucius, and nearly a thousand years after he was dead.   This belongs to modern "Confucian Cosmogony."

---

* 盤古.
† 葛洪, 枕中書.

The *Confucian Analects* may be taken as the earliest and most authentic record of Confucius' sayings and doings. In that document we find the following evidence as to Books.

1. *The Book of Poetry* is quoted correctly (I. xv., viii., III. ii., IX. xxvi., XII. x.) five times, portions of the Book are referred to and correctly described (XVII. x., III. xx., VIII. xv., XI. v., XV. x, IX. xiv., XVII. xviii.) seven times, and the number of Odes is given roundly as 300 (II. ii.), nearly correct. Both Confucius and his disciples were quite familiar with this Book, so also was Mencius. They seem to have committed it to memory.

2. *The Book of History* is quoted differently from the one we have now, and without point (II. xxi., XIV. xliii.), only twice. On the only other passage which might be taken for a quotation (XX. i.) Dr. Legge, who did not then think Yaou and Shun mythical but historical emperors (*ti*), says, "The first five paragraphs here are mostly compiled from different parts of the *Book of History*. But there are many variations of language. The compiler may have thought it sufficient if he gave the substance of the original in his quotations, without seeking to observe a verbal accuracy, or possibly, the *Book of History*, as it was in his days may have contained the passages as he gives them, and the variations be owing to the burning of most of the Classical books by the founder of the Ts'in dynasty, and their recovery and restoration in a mutilated state. We do not find this address of Yaou to Shun in the *Book of History* Pt. I., but the different sentences may be gathered from Pt. II. ii. 14, 15, where we have the charge of Shun to Yu. Yaou's reign commenced B.C. 2356, and after reigning 73 years, he resigned his administration to Shun. He died B.C. 2256, and two years after, Shun occupied the throne, in obedience to the will of the people." Reader, you are free to believe all the History of that ancient time *if you can.*

3. *Defective Records.* "The Master said, I am able to describe the ceremonies of the Hea dynasty, but K'i cannot sufficiently attest my words, I am able to describe the ceremonies of the Yin dynasty, but Sung cannot sufficiently attest my words. They cannot do so because of the insufficiency of their records and wise men. If those were sufficient, I could adduce them in support of my words " (III. ix.). That is to say, as it was, no body would believe him; and no wonder, when he had no documentary evidence to adduce.

4. *The Yih* is once mentioned (VII. xvi.). Whether Confucius was superstitious enough to make the remark here attributed to him or not, which I very much doubt, it is evident to every one who examines the Book now called the *Yih-king*, that *it* could not have

been in existence in the time of Confucius. And what did exist even Confucius himself had not studied, and did not discourse about.

5. *Rules of Propriety.* "The Master's frequent themes of discourse were, the *Odes*, the *History*, and the maintenance of the *Rules of Propriety*" (VII. xvii.). What these last were we can only gather from the *Analects*, because the three voluminous collections of *Rules of Propriety* are of a much later date than Confucius. Mencius quotes from a *Book of Rules*, but not from any of those we have now. It is time for western scholars to give up repeating that the *Chow-li*, or *Rites of Chow*, is an authentic book. Even Chu-tsze, who was fascinated by its really absurd ceremonial, and imagined it must have come down from Chow-kung, was obliged, to confess that Mencius could not have seen it :—孟子是不見周禮 *Chu-tzse's Works* § xxxvii.

13　12　11　10　9　8　7　6　5　4　3　2　1

傷神

正名引句　生前神魂○此神字與心字魂字性字皆畧通用與靈字不通用

1　李山甫詩　眼前何事不傷神

2　干逖詩　感念傷我神

3　文秀寫眞詩　圖形期自見自見却傷神

4　温庭筠詩　紅粉自傷神

5　羅隱詩　一種山前路入秦萬山堪愛此傷神

6　又　逼臉橫頤咽復勻也曾讒毀也傷神

7　別賦　感寂寞而傷神

8　喻鳧詩　那復傷神所河昏落日間

9　姚合詩　見說忘情惟有酒夕陽對酒更傷神

10　陳標詩　斷崖冰滑恐傷神

11　鮑溶詩　楚童胡爲傷我神

12　曹鄴詩　剪妾身上巾贈郞傷妾神

13　高適詩　行矣勿復言歸歟傷我神

28 27 26 25 24 23 22 21 20 19 18 17 16 15 14

役神

勞神

淮南子卷十六 有言則傷其神之神者

杜甫詩 不覺老夫神內傷

晉陽秋 荀粲婦病亡未殯傅嘏往唁粲不哭而神傷

牟融詩 十年學道苦勞神

魏徵上十思疏 何必勞神苦思

唐方干詩 坐看孤峭却勞神

雲笈七籤 食穀者多智而勞神

李紳詩 飛春走月勞神昏

莊子 寠人勞君之神與形

李中詩 卷舒惟合道喜慍不勞神

杜光庭詩 不能勞神傚蘇生張生兮

又 不能勞神傚楊朱墨翟兮

姚合詩 失寢覺神勞

方干詩 日夜役神多損壽

顧甄遠詩 役盡心神銷盡骨

番号	題	出典	例文
29		僧皎然詩	形靜神不役
30	苦神	楚辭九章	愁歎苦神靈遙思兮
31	逼神	白居易詩	只有一身宜愛惜少教冰炭逼心神
32	損神	陸翽詩·	沈憂損神慮
33		劉乂詩	益我貨者損我神
34		道德經註	損神終日談虛空不必歸於我胎中、我神不西亦不東、
35	損性靈	譚用之詩	坐掩衡茅損性靈
36	費神	呂氏春秋	單唇乾肺質神傷魂
37	神疲	蘇軾詩	貧賤苦形勞富貴曉神疲
38	神倦	拾遺記	浮提國獻神通善書善畫二人佐老子撰道德經晝夜精勤、
39		釋善生客情詩	形勞神倦
40	病神	武元衡詩	畜恨霜侵鬢搜詩病入神
41	憐神	項斯聞蟬詩	事往憐神魄　動葉復驚神
42	驚神	杜甫詩	把君詩過日念此別驚神

57	56	55	54	53	52	51	50	49	48	47	46	45	44	43
神昏	神喪	神愚	竦神				悵神					駭神		

43 舒元輿詩　願堅容足分莫使獨驚神

44 許棠題金山寺詩　四面波濤匝中樓日月鄰上窺如出世下瞰忽驚神

45 琴賦　竦衆聽而駭神

46 姚合看蓮詩　乍見神應駭

47 又得新詩　得處神應駭

48 別賦　使人意奪神駭

49 張祐居玉潭詩　神駭玉光沉

50 洛神賦　忽不悟其所舍悵神宵而蔽光

51 牟融詩　十年飄泊如萍跡一度登臨一悵神

52 高適詩註　不知何日方還徒令人神悵耳

53 漢書禮樂志　聽者莫不虛已竦神

54 杜甫聰馬行　夙昔傳聞思一見牽來左右神皆竦

55 兩般秋雨庵隨筆　于以知公之意狡而神愚也

56 又　直令賣骨董者神喪氣沮

57 李建勳詩　甚矣頻頻醉神昏體亦虛

71　70　　69　68　67　66　65　64　63　62　61　60　59　58

飛神　騁神　　馳神　神惕　神　聳神　　動神　昏渴神　　　亂神

賈松夏日可畏賦　仰之考目眩精耗處之者神昏體悸

荀子
酒亂其神也

劉晝子
哀樂之感不以亂神

淮南子
勞形則神亂

劉晝史詩
湘瓷泛輕花滌盡昏渴神、

曹植詩
自顧非金石咄唶令心悲心悲動我神、

孔德璋北海移文　形馳魄散志變神動]

劉禹錫觀舞詩
體輕似無骨觀者皆聳神]

李山甫詩
朱排六相助神聳、

劉禹錫詩
因話近世仙聳然心神惕、

遊天台賦
余所以馳神運思

劉禹錫詩
使我獨坐形神馳

又詩序
神馳而形閴者

琴賦
瓊蕤蘺法般倕騁神

關尹子
知夫此身如夢中物隨情所見可以飛神、

85	84	83	82	81	80	79	78	77	76	75	74	73	72
廻神	歸神	神散	盪靈	瀿神	神徙	神遷	遨神				遊神		飛靈

72（飛靈） 程頤上仁宗書
況爲患者豈止西戎臣每思之神魂飛越、

73 顏延之庭誥文
練形之家必就深曠及飛靈餞丹石粒芝精所以還年

74（遊神） 張蘊古大寶箴
縱心乎湛然之域遊神於至道之精

75 王褒九懷
登九靈兮游神

76 淮南子
身處江海之上而神遊魏闕之下

77 列子
舟車足力所不及神遊而已又韻府夢字註寐中神遊、

78（遨神） 張召祖詠懷詩
蕭條獨遨神

79（神遷） 白居易詩
貌隨歲律換神逐光陰遷

80（神徙） 淮南子
狂者形不虧神將有所遠徙

81（瀿神） 王粲七釋
亂精瀿神

82（盪靈） 江淹學梁王兎園賦
既投冠而棄劍亦抗魄而盪靈、

83（神散） 陸龜蒙
心散意散形散神散言散誕之人、

84（歸神） 淮南子
神農之作琴也以歸神

85（廻神） 孟郊詩
八風鼓太和廻我神霄輦

100	99	98	97	96	95	94	93	92	91	90	89	88	87	86
集神	會神				凝神	停神	載神	神藏				潛神	羈神	牧神

No.	出處	文
86	鶡冠子	苟精牧神、註苟、急敕也、牧驅制也、
87	呂氏春秋	故不能學者於俗羈神於世矜勢好尤、
88	蔣濟疏	陛下潛神默思
89	答賓戲	潛神默記
90	玉巖叟薦程頤疏	臣以頤抱道養德之日久、而潛神積慮之功深
91	李山甫詩	潛神却入黃庭閑、 閉塞不顯也
92	連珠	神藏於形、雖近則密、
93	雲笈七籤	形者載神之車也
94	司空曙詩	烟霞高占寺、楓竹暗停神、
95	莊子	用志不分乃凝於神
96	歐陽詹詩	青窗朱戶半天開、極目凝神望幾迴、
97	高蟾詩	洞庭山崒晚凝神
98	李山甫詩	瞑坐神凝萬象空
99	聖主得賢臣頌	聚精會神得益章
100	關尹子	神不外馳可以集神

115 114 113 112 111 110 109 108 107 106 105 104 103 102 101

番号	詞	出典	引文
101	定神	班固竹扇賦	安體定神達消息
102	靜神	杜光庭詩	靜神凝思仰青冥
103		雲笈七籤	神靜而心和心和而形全
104		又	神靜意平
105		韓非子	神靜則少費
106		張融答周顒書	神靜而道二吾未之聞也
107	神恬	劉勰新論	神恬心清則形無累矣
108	神閒	賈島詩	獨自南齋臥神閒景亦空
109		儲光羲詩	但見神色閒中心如虛空
110	安神	後漢書仲長統傳	安神閨房思老氏之玄虛呼吸精和求至人之彷彿
111	寧神	法言	孝莫大於寧親寧親莫大於寧神
112	淨神	春秋繁露	君子平意以淨神淨神以養氣
113	清神	司空圖詩	倦行今白首歸臥已清神
114		僧皎然詩	朝輝爍我肌賢士清我神
115		又	再飲清我神

130　129　128　127　126　125　124　123　122　121　120　119　118　117　116

孔神　　通神　休神　釋神　　　放神　疏神　　澄神

130　楚辭遠遊　一氣孔神註專已心也、　於中夜存註恒在身也、

129　天隱子　信定閒慧四門通神謂之神解

128　武帝內傳　今且與汝靈光先生經可以通神

127　神仙傳　美色淑姿幽閒娛樂不致思慾之惑所以通神也、

126　淮南子　事其神者神去之、　註其神者神居之、　註事治也、

125　莊子　解心釋神漠然無魂

124　楚辭遠遊　神要眇以淫放　註魂魄漂然而遠征也

123　雲笈七籤　兀然放神使心如枯木身如委衣、

122　蘇舜欽詩　邦國方登俊江湖且放神

121　中論　學也者所以疏神達思怡情理性聖人之上務也、

120　摯虞愍騷　泰則擄志於宇宙否則澄神於幽昧

119　曹植七啟　離俗澄神定靈

118　李中詩　尋師來靜境神骨覺淸涼

117　僧貫休詩　神淸尋夢在香極覺花新、

116　李羣玉詩　氣爽神清刻骨聰、

145　144　143　142　141　140　139　138　137　136　135　134　133　132　131

保靈　保神　　抱神　持神　垂神　　　　　　　留神　　用神

韓非子　衆人之用神也躁、聖人之用神也靜、

參同契　夫人晝明則用魂用神

杜牧詩　憲宗皇帝亦留神　秦疏多有

包拯論委任大臣疏　陛下留神

匡衡治性正蒙疏　願陛下少留神明

洛神賦　足往神留

文賦　六情底滯志往神留

曹植求通親表　冀陛下儻發天聰而垂神聽也、

蔡邕釋誨　樂天知命持神休已、

莊子　體性抱神

文　抱神以聽

莊子　抱神以靜形將自正

神仙傳　修性以保神

又　形體保神各有儀則謂之性

蔡邕瞽枕銘　應龍蟠蟄潛德保靈、

160	159	158	157	156	155	154	153	152	151	150	149	148	147	146
頤神	養性靈				養神	神肅	神重	適神			嗇神			存神

晉書曹毗傳	傅咸傳	王績詩	劉禹錫詩	曹唐詩	左傳	鮑溶詩	李郢詩	王吉	後漢書周盤傳	李康運命論	權德輿詩	司空圖	白居易詩	班固幽通志賦

虞公潛崇岩以頤神、梁生適南越以保真。

靜默頤神、

此日長昏飲非關養性靈、

玉城山裏多靈藥擺落功名且養神、

常向羅浮保養神、

敬在養神

禮餘神轉肅

骨清須貴達神重有威儀

專意積精以適神

周能感親嗇神養福

不愛其身而嗇其神、

孝理本憂勤立功在嗇神、

神存富貴始輕黃金

存神機慮息養氣語言遲、

守寂寞而存神

174	173	172	171	170	169	168		167	166	165	164	163	162	161
爽神	悅神		怡神			暢神		娛性靈	娛神	熙神	調神	融神	和神	

右（161〜167）：

161 和神　魏書崔浩傳
陛下可以優游無爲頤神養壽、

162 融神　漢書田千秋傳
玩聽音樂養志和神、

163 調神　皇甫松大隱賦序
是可以融神保和含道詠德、

164 熙神　唐明皇送司馬承禎詩
林泉先得性芝桂欲調神、

165 娛神　梁冀傳
高枕熙神、

166 娛神　舞賦
天王燕胥樂而不佚娛神遺老永平之術、

167 娛性靈　漢書外戚傳
無涓共和娛靈保林𡱈使夜者皆視百石　註娛靈
可以娛樂情靈也、

左（168〜174）：

168 暢神　劉琨詩
音以賞奏味以珠珍文以明言言以暢神、

169 怡神　皮日休詩
怡神時高吟

170　歡逝賦
生而不喜死而不慼瑤臺夏屋不能悅其神、

171 怡神　劉峻辨命論
神何適而獲怡

172　長門賦
登蘭臺而遙望兮神悅悅而外淫　註遊也、

173 悅神　成文幹詩
爽神猻露滴樓臺、

174 爽神　賈島詩
池滿風生竹時時得爽神、

188 187 186 185　　184 183 182 181 180 179　178 177 176 175

神變　神洋洋　　神王　神高　丰神　神麗

175 常建聽琴詩　一指指應法、一聲聲爽神、

176 李羣玉詩　雲天入掌握爽朗神魂淨、

177 王仁裕詩　骨清神爽似聞韶

178 六朝宗文　汝神意爽悟

179 神麗　固以自然神麗而足思願愛樂矣

180 丰神　琴賦　丰神卓越

181 尸牘碎錦　南威不敢鬪丰神

182 神高　張淮詩　神高得詩思

183 李羣玉詩　來此多沈醉神高無宿醒

184 神王　姚合題河亭詩

185 莊子　澤雉十步一啄、百步一飲、不蘄畜乎樊中、神雖王不善也

186 唐朱逵詩　連飲百杯神轉王

187 神洋洋　李咸用詩　亂流直涉神洋洋

188 神變　周繇詩　色授應難奪神變願莫辭、

溫庭筠詩　神變花冉冉眉語柳毿毿

189 190 191　192　153　154 195 196 197 198

入神　神色　徵神　形神　心神

夏侯孝東方朔畫贊　棄俗登仙神交造化
更無外事來心肺空有清虛入思神
晉書王戎傳
戎年六七歲於宣武場觀戲猛獸在檻中虎吼眾皆奔
走戎獨立不動神色自若

又王獻之傳
然
嘗與徽之共坐一室忽然火發徽之遽走獻之神色恬

目
明達之色夫色見於貌所謂徵神徵神見貌則情發於

劉邵九徵
故誠仁必有溫柔之色誠勇必有矜奮之色誠智必有

稽康養生論
服食養身使形神相親
東都賦
形神寂寞耳目弗營
姚合詩
顒顒其形神

魏書釋老志
其為教也鏑去邪累澡雪心神
○人生前多說神明

佛書
夫神者我也形者我所舍也

神明
明

朱子全書心
然心之體用始終雖有真妄邪正之分其實莫非神明
不測之妙

知者心之神明

韓非子
食穀者智慧而巧食氣者神明而壽

漢書
鍊魂抱魄心開神明

諺語
潔其宮開其門去私毋言神明若存

管子
耳目司其官神明守其舍

雲笈七籤
賈逵五歲神明過人

大戴禮
空竅者神明之戶牖也耳目竭於聲色精神竭於外貌

胡敬齋
故中無主此言神明之不離其實也

鶡冠子
性情不鍊則神明不發

劉勰
近而至故謂之神遠而反故謂之明
為神神之在器者為明
　　註明之在道者

精神
神

○精神與魂畧同

吳越春秋
楚王見歐冶子之三劍精神大悦

219　218　　217　　216　215　214　213　212　211　　210

潛靈　神逝

謝枋得交信錄序　天下達道不曰朋友而曰朋友之交交者精神有契、道德有同非外相慕也

莊子　五味者須精神之運心術之動然後從之者也、

又　其寐也魂交其覺也形開、　註魂交者精神交錯也、

淮南子精神　精神馳騁於外而不守則禍福之至雖如邱山無由識之矣

鮑溶詩　金泥舞虎精神暗銀鏤交龍氣色寒

郭鈺詩　幾回夢想玉精神

釋修睦詩　長空秋雨歇睡起覺精神

又　有精而不使有神而不行、　註不濁其精不勞其神

又　死後神魂　○此神字與魂字靈字鬼字皆累通用或稱精神或稱靈

神逝　楚辭遠遊　神儵忽而不返兮形枯槁而獨留、　註、魂靈速逝遊四維也　魂亦有

潛靈　寡婦賦　潛靈邈其不返兮

231　230　229　　228　227　226　225　224　223　222　221　220

精　魂　神　　遷　　　　　神　　　　靈　歸
神　乘　升　　神　　　　　神　　　　魂　神

謝惠連祭古冢文　曜質幾年潛靈幾歲、

王僧達祭顏光祿文　秋露未凝歸神太素、

李縱置酒行詩　安得凌風羽崦嵫駐靈魂無然坐衰老黯歎東陵柏

關尹子　靈魂為賢屬魄為愚

東方朔七諫　何山石之嶄巖兮靈魂屈而偃蹇、

寡婦賦　將遷神而安厝　註將葬

又　神一夕而九升

魏文帝寡婦詩　思君魂一夕而九乘

詩經大雅　文王陟降在帝左右、　又三后在天、　朱子註其精神上與天合也　又性理大全正蒙註非謂吾死猶有精靈不亡、

成語考　傳說死其精神託於箕尾　火燒其宗廟器者哀精神之有虧傷

禮記檀弓註

宋羅願淳安縣社壇記　君民之情如此其同也以其生有平土植穀之能灼知其精神死不泯滅

232 爲神　册聞錄

死而爲神再世爲人者有之

233 夢神　白居易詩

夜夢歸長安見我故親友損之在我左順之在我右又神合俄頃間神離欠伸後覺來疑在側求索一無有

234 靈夢　劉兼詩

再取素琴聊假寐南柯靈夢莫相通

205 交神　應德璉正情賦

魂翩翩而夕遂夜同夢而交神

236 交靈　蔡邕撿逸賦

晝聘情以舒愛抵夢以交靈

237 致神　白居易長恨歌序

楊妃死皇悲甚三年其念不衰求之魂夢杳不能得適有道士自蜀來知上皇心念楊妃如是自言有李某之術明皇大喜命致其神

238 神象　姚向諸葛丞相廟詩

執簡焚香入廟門武侯神象儼如存

239 神依　册聞錄

陸射山徵君夢尊人孝廉公云吾窆穿內爲水所浸甚苦皐亭山頂有地一區召售無人曷往買之而移葬於此吾神所依也

240 小鬼之神　前漢書

杜主故周之右將軍其在秦中最小鬼之神也師古曰其鬼雖小而有神靈也

靈慧神妙

番号	標目	出典	引文
253	最愚而靈	漢書刑法志	夫人肖天地之貌懷五常之性聰明精碎有生之最靈
252	萬物之靈	書經	惟人萬物之靈
251	愚而神	春秋胡傳僖公九年	民至愚而神
250	神器	老子	天下神器不可爲也、　註器物也、人乃天下之神物也、
249	最神	管子註	天下人心最神
248	暢靈	孔融與曹操書	高祖非醉斬白蛇無以暢其靈、
247	克靈	書經	不克靈承於旅
246	克神	張衡綏筍銘	垂光厥世子孫克神、
245	爲靈	左傳襄公二年	君子是以知齊靈公之爲靈也
244	爲神	尙友姓氏譜	有村巫以銀甖貯二蛇惑民觀者塞路陸起斬蛇捕巫、遠近駭服稱爲神明、
243	有靈	李羣玉	顧氏傳神寶有靈
242	有神	韓文公	薛公庶幾有神
241	有神	杜甫詩	將軍畫善蓋有神

267　266　265　264　263　262　261　260　259　258　257　256　255　254

用靈　赫靈　聲靈　靈微　　　　　　　　　精靈　心靈　懷靈　禀靈

者也

【254　禀靈】宋書謝靈運傳論　民禀天地之靈含五常之德、

【255　懷靈】又　禀氣懷靈理無或異
陶弘景葛公碑　懷靈抱識之士、知杳冥之有精焉、

【256　心靈】隋書經籍志　詩者所以導達心靈歌咏情志者也、

【257　精靈】荀悦高祖讚　焚魚斬蛇異功同符豈非精靈之感哉、
江淹詩　精靈歸妙理
杜甫詩　哀詔惜精靈
又　交期余潦倒材力爾精靈
李德林天命論　氣調精靈括囊宇宙
禮記祭義註　識從氣生性則神出入也、故人之精靈謂之神、

【264　靈微】司空圖詩　匪神之靈匪機之微、

【265　聲靈】詩經　赫赫厥聲濯濯厥靈

【266　赫靈】又　以赫厥靈

【267　用靈】書經　苗民弗用靈

| 280　279 | 278　277　276　275　274　273 | 272　271　270　269　268 |

丕靈
又
丕靈承帝事

藉靈
左傳宣公十二年　敢藉君靈以濟楚師、

假靈
又昭公三十二年　我欲徼福假靈於成王

乞靈
又哀公二十四年　寡君欲徼福於周公乞靈於臧氏

託靈
北史魏彭城王勰傳　上於布衣猶爲知己盡命況臣託靈先皇誠應竭股肱之力

賴靈
史記秦始皇本紀　賴陛下神靈明聖

以君之靈
左傳僖公二十八年　以君之靈不有寧也、

王之神
國策　今國者王之叢勢者王之神

君之神
管子　禮義者人君之神也、

神威
唐書　改殿前左右射生軍爲左右神威軍、

楊萬里論神威疏　臣聞聖人之伸於天下也有神而其屈於天下也有威威藏於神故其威不測神行於威故其神不狎、

韓非子　主上不神下將有因、

又　主失其神虎隨其後

281 靈威
南史論
武帝靈威薄霞重關自闢英籌所包先勝而后戰也、

282 靈威
晋書樂志正旦大會歌
邁洪化振靈威懷萬方納九夷、

283 神監
任彥昇徐南洲行狀
體睿履正神監淵邈、

284 神撼
李德裕題學士院句
銀花懸院榜神撼引鈴絲、

285 神伏
羅隱詩
由來四皓須神伏大抵秦皇謾氣強、

286 伏靈
鼎錄
山伏其靈海伏其異、

287 神不可傳
陸士衡連珠
耳無嘗音之察、目無照影之神、垂於世者可繼、止於身者難結、是以元晏之風恆存、動神之化已滅、 註元晏

288 神專
周禮春官瞽矇註
瞽者其神不在耳而專在目、瞽者其神不在目而專在耳、批此言法可傳神不可傳、禮教也、

289 得神
李白草書歌行註
旭言始吾見公主擔夫爭路而得筆法之意、後見公孫氏舞劍而得其神、

290 得神
兩般秋雨庵隨筆
戰國養士論陳同甫上孝宗書皆得太史公之神、

291 傳神
蘇軾題畫竹詩
老可能為竹寫真小坡今與竹傳神、

305　304　303　302　301　300　299　298　297　296　295　294　293　　292

通靈　　　　通　入　　　入　寫
　　　　　　神　靈　　　神　神

蔡邕中題莊子序
善繪者傳其神、善書者模其意、莊子傳老氏之神、模

九經之意

唐書選舉志
言辭俯仰之間侍郎非通神不可、

習鑿齒長鳴雞賦
嘉鳴雞之合德、智窮神而入靈、

劉勰新論
是故學者必精勤專心以入於神、

曹植
奇文美藝通微入神

易經
精義入神以致用也

長笛賦
是故可以通靈感物寫神喻意

管子
變化通於鬼神

幽閑鼓吹
錢至十萬可以通神矣

杜甫李潮八分歌
苦縣光和尚骨立書貴瘦硬方通神、

幽通賦
精通靈而感物兮神動氣而入微、

隋書皇甫績傳
握符受籙合極通靈

藝術傳
咸詣幽微思侔造化通靈入妙、殊才絕技、

北史尉元傳
至孝通靈至順感幽

318	317	316	315	314	213	312		311	310	309	308	307	306
酒有神			神物	神駿		神勇		神似	神妙	神化			望神

世說

玉局講殘春換刧、石臺丹在草通靈、
卽寫望之神情也、

王績詩註

淮南子繆稱

心之精者可以神化、而不可以導人、

杜甫觀曹將軍畫馬詩 國初巳來畫鞍馬神妙獨數江都王

兩般秋雨庵隨筆 我生平觀臨松雪書者多矣、未見有如此神似者、

桓豹奴是王丹陽外甥、形似其舅宣武云不恒相似、時

似耳恒似是形時似是神桓逾不悅

南史梁始與忠武王憺傳 吏人嘆服咸稱神勇

唐書劉黑闥傳 每乘隙奮奇兵出不意多所摧克軍中號為神勇、

拾遺記 曹洪所乘馬足似不踐地時人謂乘風而行亦一代神駿、

易經 是與神物以前民用

孟郊詩 天生此神物為我洗憂患、

秦觀飲酒詩 花下本無俗酒中別有神、

性理大全正蒙註 糟粕有時可見乃成酒者而酒之為味為用、則若神
焉

330　329　328　327　　326　325　324　323　322　321　320　　319a　319

酒神

茶神

花神

羣神

謂神

英靈

聖神

・

聖靈

生靈

靈物

靈物

李德裕文章論

譬諸日月、雖終古常見、而光景常新此所以爲靈物也、

尚友姓氏譜

扁鵲曰長兄於病視神未有形而除之

生靈

人

拯生靈之塗炭

聖靈

唐西平王碑

聖靈昔廻眷微尚不及宜、註聖靈謂高祖也、

謝靈運詩

聖靈閔頑嚚、註皇上閔下民也、

韓文公

庶聖靈之饗像想幽神之復光

聖神

弔魏武帝詩

聖神功化之極

中庸

聖神無隱者

英靈

王維詩

英靈盡來歸

謂神

天隱子

人生時稟得靈氣精明通悟學無滯塞則謂之神

宅神於內遺昭於外自然異於俗人則謂之神仙

羣神

思元賦

從伯禹稽山嘉羣神之執玉兮、　註神臣也、

花神

異人錄

宋單父種花萬本色樣各殊人呼爲花神、

茶神

全唐詩話

陸鴻漸撰茶經三卷世目爲茶神、

酒神

海錄碎事

酒席之上九吐而不減其量者爲酒神、

331 錢神

韋莊詩

亂來知酒聖貧去覺錢神

332 皇帝

書經

皇帝哀矜庶戮之不辜

333

楚辭遠遊章句

軒轅不可攀援兮註皇帝以往難攀引也、軒轅皇帝也

334

史記秦始皇紀

始作車服天下號之為軒轅氏也

臣等謹與博士議曰古有天皇有地皇有泰皇泰皇最

貴臣等昧死上尊號王為泰皇王曰去泰著皇采上古

帝位號號曰皇帝　此中國君生前稱皇帝之始自有

國以來約千餘年所未有亦孔孟所未聞也、

335 黃帝

兩般秋雨庵隨筆吟荆軻詩　鳴呼天意帝秦不可回

336

易經

黃帝堯舜垂衣裳而天下治

337

禮記

中央土其日戊已其帝黃帝

338

幽通賦

黃神貌而靡質兮　註黃帝作夢書

339 黃神

淮南子卷六

西老折勝黃神嘯吟　註黃帝之神傷也

340

思元賦

黃靈詹而訪命兮　註黃帝也

341 黃靈

列子楊朱篇

太古之事滅矣孰誌之哉三皇之事若存若亡五帝之

349 348 347 ´　　　346 345 344 343 342 ´

三　二　　　　　巨　陰　九　圓
靈　靈　　　　　靈　靈　靈　靈

晉　宋　獨　　　王　劉　楚　張　｜
書　史　孤　　　維　禹　　載　物
　　樂　及　　　華　錫　辭　月
　　志　仙　　　嶽　　　　賦
　　　　掌
　　　　銘

事若覺若夢

地物也天神也、又地對天不過

桑祇雪凝圓靈水鏡　註天也

登九靈　註九天也

陰靈既望圓　註月也

西嶽出浮雲積雪在太清連天凝黛色百里遙青冥白

日爲之寒森沈華陰城昔聞乾坤閉造化生巨靈右足

踏方止左手推削成天地忽開拆大河注東溟遂爲西

峙嶽雄鎮秦京大君包覆載至德被羣生上帝佇昭

告金天思奉迎人祇望幸久何獨禪云亭

帝命巨靈經啟地脈

際天蟠地默運二靈

道貫三靈　註天地人也、

日月星亦稱三靈

361	360	359	358	357	356	355	354	353	352	351	350
上神	上帝	土龍芻狗帝	龜神	骨神	泥木神	扶靈	芻靈	大靈	五靈	四靈	三神
又用兵	大戴禮成德	淮南子 中國所事神	述異記	雍裕之詩	俗例	俗例		禮記	韓文公	禮記	甘泉賦

三神 註天地人也

麟鳳龜龍謂之四靈

赤靈黃靈青靈白靈黑靈五方之靈物也

大靈頓頭、註大靈龜也、

塗車芻靈自古有之、註芻靈束茅爲人馬謂之靈者、神之類、

扶神主牌轎杠曰扶靈

即泥木偶像也

道士年已至仙家鳥亦來骨爲神不朽、眼向故人開、

鯉魚滿三百六十鱗蛟龍輒率而飛去一年置一神守之則不能去矣神則龜也、

譬若旱歲之土龍疾疫之芻狗是時爲帝者也、

升聞皇天上帝歆焉、

升聞皇天上神歆焉、

374　373　372　371　370　369　368　367　366　365　364　363　362

374	373	372	371	370	369	368	367	366	365	364	363	362
五上帝	天靈		高靈	蒼靈	蒼神	穹靈	至神					上靈
史記封禪書	吳越春秋	韓愈	朱子詩	春秋元命苞	北史魏閔帝紀	北史魏明帝紀	楊子問神篇註	沈休文碑文	顏延之詩	梁武帝祠南郊詔	禮記禮運	孔子家語

362：以降上神、註上神天也、

363：以降上神、註上神天神也又在上精魂之神、

364：恭祗明祀昭事上靈

365：思對上靈之心

366：河岳之上靈

367：天有至神為造化之主聖人之神為道之宗其神一也、

368：穹靈降祉麟趾泉繁

369：上協蒼靈之慶下昭后祇之錫、

370：殷時五星聚於房房者蒼神之精周據而興、

371：稽首仰高靈

372：高靈下墜、註高靈謂天神之有靈者

373：蒙天靈之祐神祇之福、

374：高祖入關間故秦時上帝祠何帝也對曰四帝有白青黃赤帝之祠高祖曰吾聞天有五帝而有四何也莫知其說於是高祖曰吾知之矣乃待吾而具五也乃立黑

383　382 391 380　379　378 377 376 375

五神

十上帝

八神

三十二上帝　又

三十六上帝

李白

謝朓雩祭歌

史記封禪書

史記武帝紀
帝祠命曰北畤
天神貴者泰一泰一佐曰五帝　註五帝五天帝也
梁簡文帝吳興楚王神廟碑　昔者武王詢於太公五神之禮
漢樂章五神歌
周禮太宰朱子註　五神相包四鄰土地廣楊浮雲

周禮上帝是總言帝五帝是五方帝昊天上帝是天
鄭氏以昊天上帝爲北極非也北極星只是言天之象
又漢時大乙便是帝如今郊祀增成十帝一國三公尚
不可況天而有十帝乎

八神一曰天主二曰地主三曰兵主四曰陰主五曰陽
主六曰月主七曰日主八曰時主

璧七曜詔八神排閶闔渡天津

玉京註玉京無爲之天也三十二帝之都

三十六帝註道書有三十六天上帝東方八天云云三
十六名都齊載
今世俗所奉者則玉皇上帝　立霄高上帝　玉清上

384 三十六玉皇 又

385 十六神 星經

386 諸天上帝 李白

387 諸天神 周禮天官

388 萬帝 吳筠詩

389 萬神 道書齊丘子

390 萬靈 趙光逢詩

391 萬靈 史記

帝、玉辰上帝、伏魔上帝、協天上帝即關帝、

三元上帝即三官、雷祖上帝、妙無上帝即太清老

子、立天上帝、南方上帝、太乙上帝、此其大槩

也、

為君持此凌蒼蒼上朝三十六玉皇、註即三十六天

帝、

太乙乃天使之神主使十六神知風雨水旱兵革饑饉

疾疫、

靈書註靈書度人經此二章並是諸天上帝及至靈魔

王隱秘之音

掌建邦之天神人鬼地示之禮

隱符千魔駭鳴玉萬帝悅

萬物一物也萬神一神也斯道之至矣、

應天命擁神休萬靈感百祿遒

黃帝接萬靈明廷明廷甘泉也

406　405　404　403　402　401　400　399　398　397　396　395　394　393　392

神靈　　有靈　有靈　　百靈　百神　　百神　　衆靈　羣靈　羣神　羣帝

杜甫詩
玉京羣帝集北斗

書堯典
偏于羣神

鄭獬賦
偏羣靈以從之、祀嚴太祖以爲之侑、

李商隱詩
上帝鈞天會衆靈

詩周頌
懷柔百神及河喬嶽

鶡冠子
以是知先靈王百神者　先靈先王之靈

隋書高祖紀
和百靈而利萬民

書經
惟爾有神尚克相予

管子註
每大陵深溪皆有靈

今古奇觀
願父母有靈敢牖二第

韓文公
郊天告廟神靈歡喜風雨明晦無不從順、

又
神靈日歆歆　註言山谷鳴吼如神靈也、

魯靈光殿賦
神靈扶其棟宇千載

班固
襲四宗之緝熙神靈

楊雄諫不受單于朝書　神靈之所想望

418	417	416	415	414	413	412	411	410 409 408 407
祭上帝		髮神	腦目鼻舌神	頑神	湘靈	湘神		河靈　河神
書經	神仙傳	道書黃庭經解	海錄碎事　酉陽雜俎	李咸用石版詩	楚辭	李賀帝子歌	蔡襄詩	楊雄河東賦　汪尊西河詩　匡衡政治得失疏

匡衡政治得失疏　神靈應而嘉祥見

廟鼓賽河神

河靈颶踢爪華蹈衰

花貌年年溺水濱俗傳河伯娶生人自從明宰投巫後、

直至如今見不神

湘神彈琴迎帝子

當庭卓立凝頑神

使湘靈鼓琴兮

腦神曰覺元目神曰虛監鼻神曰沖龍王舌神曰始梁、

髮神曰玄華

有眼神鼻神口神齒神舌神其神甚多不可數計又八萬四千毫毛亦皆化為護法神

人受精養體服氣煉形則萬神自守其眞不然者則榮衞枯悴萬神自逝

肆類于上帝　朱子註先祭上帝、

No.	名	出典	文
419	祭神	又	偏于羣神　孔穎達曰、祭法云、有天下者祭百神、偏祭
420	祭靈	韓文公	祭于亡友柳子厚之靈
421	祭神	又	祭于仰山之神、又祭于城隍之神、
422	祭靈	又	禱告于城隍神之靈
423	禮上帝	管子	將以禮上帝
424	禮神	唐詩	漢帝精神禮百神
425	禮靈	禮記	禮靈之符藏之宗廟
426	尊神	鶡冠子	殷人尊神率民以事神
427	尊靈	齊書樂志	報惟事天祭實尊靈
428	上帝臨	詩經	上帝臨汝
429	神格	又	神之格思
430	降神	又	惟嶽降神生甫及申　註、言嶽山高大而降其神靈和氣以生甫侯申伯
431	降靈	晉書文明皇后傳	海岱降靈

443	442	441	440	439	438	437	436	435	434	433	372
惡神	鬼帝		為靈	為神	託神		感靈	靈啟	天啟	神	感

神感

張茂先勵志詩

沈亞之賢良方正策　殷宗之極誠於神、神感於夢而得傳說、

蒲盧縈繳神感飛禽、注蒲且子見雙鳥過之其不被

弋者亦下、故云感也、

天啟

徐陵為陳武帝下州郡璽書　豈曰人謀皆由天啟、

靈啟

張華詩

靈啟其願邀願在茲于以表情爰著斯詩、

感靈

齊書樂志

禮以昭事樂以感靈

曹植七啟

夫辯言之豔能使窮澤生流枯木發榮庶感靈而激神、

託神

道德經序

老子託神李母剖左掖而生、

為神

俗語

人生而正直死而為神

為靈

悒聞錄

生而為英死而為靈

生而正故死而靈

又

五方五鬼帝之姓名皆在

鬼帝

葛洪枕中書

邪神

惡神

史記

始皇夢與海神戰問占夢博士曰此惡神當除去而善

神可致、

454　453　442　451　450　　449　448　　447　446　445　444

犯　煞　癘　神　　厲　旱　　猛　淫　姦　凶
神　神　神　崇　　神　神　　神　神　神　神

又　中　兩　又　說　　楚　詩　　論　風　國　姚
　　國　般　　文　　辭　小　　衡　俗　語　合
　　通　秋　　　　　九　雅　　　　通　　　惡
　　書　雨　　　　　章　　　　　　怪　　　神
　　　　庵　　　　　　　　　　　　神　　　行
　　　　隨　　　　　　　　　　　　　　　　雨
　　　　筆　　　　　　　　　　　　　　　　詩

凶神扁簸惡神行

神無間行、註間行、姦神淫厲之屬、

二世欲解淫神

宅中主神十有二焉、靑龍白虎、列十二位龍虎猛神、天
之正鬼也

旱魃爲虐　註魃旱神也

昔予夢登天兮、魂中道而無杭、吾使厲神占之兮曰有
志極而無旁　註厲神殤鬼也

祟神禍也臣鍇曰禍者人之所召也神因而附之

亦癘神無故而爲

李赤自比李白後爲厠神所祟而死見柳子厚集、

煞神每年在一方如在東方則日大殺東方凡欲修建
地方者若該地向東方此年不可修建避神煞也、

有六十花甲犯神犯之則病四肢不安須用果酒送之
方愈名曰起犯犯神每日午後下降故起犯必須午後、

462	461	460	459	458	457	456	455
神附	祭醼	殺神附	祀鬼	祀神	祭醼	殺神	神罪

455 神罪

李善夷賣漢水　見唐詩
天子禮之必有其神楚人膠其船而禍其君、神不能福神之罪也、

456 殺神

周禮秋官壺涿氏
若欲殺其神則以牡樺午貫象齒而沈之、則其神死、

457 祀鬼

禮記註
鬼有所歸乃不爲厲以其無歸或爲人害故祀之、

458 祀神

周禮地官
春秋祭醼註醼者爲人物裁害之神也、

459 祭醼

粤東筆記
安崖有二司神者一日降魂童言曰欲與蕭公闘法於

是二司神各發馬脚馬脚者神所附之人也、

460 殺神附

朱子全書禮三
今世鬼神之附著生人而說話者甚多亦有祖先降神於其子孫者又如今之師巫亦有降神者蓋皆其氣類之相感所以神附著之也

461 祭醼

齊丘子
魑魅附巫祭言禍福事、每來則飲食言語皆神、每去則飲食言語皆人、不知魑魅之附巫祭也、不知巫祭之附魑魅也、

462 神附

淮南子精神註
神在男曰覡在女曰巫、

帝字雜解

鶡冠子

463 此素皇內帝之法註帝者天號王者人稱皇者天人之總美大之名

464 白虎通
帝者天號王者五行之稱也皇者何謂也亦號也皇君也美也大也　又天子夷狄
之可稱

465 詩小雅正月註

266 上帝天之神也
朱子全書禮祭註　引程子言

467 上帝即天也聚天之神而言之則謂之上帝
宋儒楊復
天帝一也星象非天天固不可以象求也以象求天是何異於知人之有形色貌象

468 而不知有心君之尊也
朱子天地
問天地之心天地之理理是道理心是主宰底意否曰心固是主宰底意然所謂主

473　472　　471　470　469

宰者、即是理也不是心外別有箇理、理外別有箇心、又間此心字與帝字相似否、曰

人字似天字心字似帝字

易經註

天之生成萬物而主宰之者謂之帝

諧聲品字箋

帝者天之宰也、天之主宰曰帝、身之主宰曰心、　又曰至靈之眞宰、

胡宏

漢祠太一求神仙方曰天神貴者太一、太一佐曰五帝、是皆不知鬼神之情狀方士家妄作儒者不取也、　又故兆於南郊埽地而祭者吳大上帝而已天言其氣帝言其性也

朱子天地

帝是理爲主

又性理二〇命

問命之不齊恐不是眞有爲之賦予如此只是二氣錯綜參差、隨其所值因各不齊、皆非人力所與故謂之天所命否曰只是從大原中流出來模樣似恁地不是眞有

爲之賦予者、那得箇人在上面分付這箇詩書所說便似有箇人在上恁地、如帝乃

震怒之類然這箇亦只是理如此天下莫尊於理故以帝名之、
又鬼神

問人之死也不知魂魄便散否、曰固是散又問子孫祭祀却有感格者如何、曰畢竟

子孫是祖先之氣他氣雖散他根却在這裏盡其誠敬則亦能呼召得他氣聚在此、

如水波檻後水非前水後波非前波然却通只是一水波子孫之氣與祖考之氣亦

是如此他那箇當下自散了然他根却在這裏根既在此又却能引聚他那氣在此、

此事難說只要人自看得問下武詩三后在天先生解云在天言其既沒而精神上

合於天此是如何、曰便是又有此理、用之云恐只是此理上合於天耳、曰既有此理、

便有此氣、或曰想是聖人稟得清明純粹之氣故其死也其氣上合於天、曰也是如

此這事又微妙難說、要人自看得世間有正當易見者、又有變化無常不可窺測者、

如此方看得這箇道理活、又如云文王陟降在帝左右、如今若說文王眞箇在上帝

左右眞箇有箇上帝、如世間所塑之像固不可、然聖人如此說便是有是理、
楚詞天問

爾曰遂古之初、誰傳道之、上下未形、何由考之、冥昭瞢闇、誰能極之、馮翼惟像、何以

識之、明明闇闇、惟時何爲、陰陽三合、何本何化、圜則九重、孰營度之、惟茲何功、孰初作之、

莊　子

天其運乎、地其處乎、日月其爭於所乎、孰主張是、孰綱維是、孰居無事而推行是、意者其有機緘而不得已耶、意者其運轉而不能自止耶、雲者爲雨乎、雨者爲雲乎、孰隆施是、孰居無事淫樂而勸是、風起北方、一西一東、有上彷徨、孰噓吸是、孰居無事而披拂是、敢問何故、　註重重微問者要人深思自得運化主宰以立君道之准、

又

若有眞宰而特不得其朕、

朱子全書　天地又諸子

或問伊川說以主宰謂之帝、孰爲主宰、曰自有主宰、蓋天是箇至剛至陽之物、自然如此運轉不息、所以如此必有爲之主宰者、這樣處要人自見得、非言語所能盡也、

因舉莊子孰綱維是孰主張是十數句、曰他也見得這道理、

又　性命

問天與命、性與理、四者之別、天則就其自然者言之、命則就其流行而賦於物者言、

483　　482　　481　　　480

之性則就其全體而萬物所得以爲生者言
之、理則就其事事物物各有其則者言
之、到得合而言之、則天即理也、命即性也、性即理也、是如此否、曰、自然但今人說天非
荅荅之謂、據某看來、亦捨不得這箇荅荅底

又　尚書

高宗夢傅說據此則是眞有箇天帝與高宗對曰吾賚汝以良弼、今人但以主宰說
帝謂無形象恐也、不得若如世間所謂玉皇大帝恐亦不可畢竟此理如何學者皆
莫能答、

文中子

帝之不帝久矣注百王稱帝者相沿前代號也、自秦始皇始、故曰不帝久矣、

又

氣爲上形爲下識都其中而三才備矣、氣爲鬼其天乎、識爲神其人乎、吾得之理性
也、

通鑑綱目　周赧王二十七年

秦以伯爵僭王亦既與周無別矣、昭襄何意思及稱帝、豈非欲以是求加於周哉、罪
孰大於此者、

莊子　卷三大宗師

夫道有情有信無爲無形可傳而不可受可得而不可見自本自根未有天地自古以固存神鬼神帝生天生地在太極之先而不爲高在六極之下而不爲深

又無古無今　歸震川批一靈長在

老子

吾不知其誰之子象帝之先

韓文公

象帝威容大註指立元也卽老子

神字　易經　集　解

帝之神、

神也者妙萬物而爲言者也註神卽帝也又帝者神之體神者帝之用又所以妙萬

又

陰陽不測之謂神

集仙錄謝自然傳

物者帝之神也

493　　492a　　492　　491　　　　　490　　489a

天上自有神非鬼神之神

朱子全書周子書
問動而無動靜而無靜曰此說動而生陽動極而靜靜而生陰靜極復動此自有箇
神在其間不屬陰不屬陽故曰陰陽不測之謂神且如晝動夜靜在晝間神不與之
俱動在夜間神不與之俱靜神又自是神神却變得晝夜晝夜却變不得神妙萬物
如說水陰根陽火陽根陰巳是有形象底是說粗底了又曰靜者為主故以蒙艮終
云

神祇　說文
天神引出萬物者也地祇提出萬物者也

字典
祇地神也

天者神也地者形也
書經羣神　蘇軾註
鵾冠子

羣神
能出雲為風雨見怪物皆曰神

501　500　499　498　497　　496　　495

左傳
神聰明正直而壹者也

管子水地龜龍類
欲小則化如蠶蠋欲大則藏於天下欲上則凌於雲氣欲下則入於深泉變化無日、

神壁
上下無時謂之神
子了

聖而不可知之謂神

知人所不知曰神
淮南子
謚法

安仁立政曰神又民無能名曰神
莊子

此謂王德之人云云
楊子雲
聖人曰神
神之又神而能精焉

507　506　505　504　503　502

又

或問神曰心請問之曰潛天而天潛地而地神明而不測者也心之潛也猶將
測之況於人乎況於事倫乎敢問潛心于聖曰昔仲尼潛心於文王矣達之顏淵亦
潛心於仲尼矣未達一間也神在所潛而已矣天神天明照知四方天精天粹萬物
作類人心其神矣乎操則存捨則亡

人之神　皇極經世

魂即神也
　朱子全書　鬼神

神人之精爽也
　朱子全書　性理

心氣之精爽
　文選和神註

神是心之至妙處
　又　道統

513　　512　　511　　510　509　　508

淮南子

心者形之主也而神者心之寶也

稽康養生論

精神之於形骸猶國之有君也神躁於中而形喪於外猶君昏於上國亂於下也、

又君子知形恃神以立神須形以存、

胡敬齋

氣之發動卽是神

總論

陳公甫

無動非神

通鑑綱目　漢明帝永平元年朝原陵註墓藏體魄而致生之是不智也劚以宅兆而致死是不仁也注死之生之謂無知與有知也又知靈也左傳子產曰人生始化曰魄旣生魄陽曰魂用物精多則魂魄强是以有精爽至於神明注人生始變化而爲形形之靈者名曰魄若視聽動運之

類魄屬陰其中自有陽氣氣之神者名曰魂如精神性識之類

又永平八年詔聽贖罪註

帝聞西域有神其名曰佛因遣使之天竺求其道得其書其書大抵以虛無爲宗貫慈悲不殺人以爲人死精神不滅隨復受形生時善惡皆有報應

朱子全書鬼神

因論魂魄鬼神之說曰只今在人便自一半是神一半是鬼了但未死以前神爲主已死之後則鬼爲主

又禮一

問氣也者神之盛也魄也者鬼之盛也豈非以氣魄未足爲鬼神氣魄之盛者乃爲鬼神否曰非也大凡說鬼神皆是通生死而言此言盛者則是指生人身上而言所以後面說骨肉斃於下陰爲野土但說魂也間頃聞先生言耳目之精明者爲魄口鼻之噓吸者爲魂以此語是而未盡耳目之所以能精明者爲魄口鼻之所以能噓吸者爲魂是箇物事形象在裏面恐如水晶相似所以發出來爲耳目之精明且如月其黑暈是魄其光是魂也想見人身魂魄也是如此人生時魂魄相交死則離而各散去魂爲陽而散上魄爲陰而降下又曰陰主藏受陽主運用凡能記憶皆魄之所藏受也至於運用發出來是魂這兩箇物事本不相離他能記憶底是魄然發出來底是魂能知覺底是魄然知覺發出來底又是魂雖

520　　　519　　　518　　517

各自分屬陰陽然陰陽中又各自有陰陽也或曰大率魄屬形體魂屬精神曰精又
是魄神又是魂　間陽魂爲神陰魄爲鬼祭義曰氣也者神之盛也魄也者鬼之盛
也而鄭氏曰氣噓吸出入者也耳目之聰明爲魄然則陰陽未可言鬼神陰陽之靈
乃鬼神也如何曰魄者形之神魂者氣之神魂魄是形氣之精英謂之靈

又　鬼神

來者爲神去者爲鬼以人身言之則氣爲神而精爲鬼

又

煖氣便是魂冷氣便是魄魂便是氣之神魄便是精之神會思量計度底便是魂會
記當去底便是魄

又

蘇氏曰物鬼也變神也鬼常與體魄俱故謂之物神無適而不可故謂之變精氣爲
魄魄爲鬼志氣爲魂魂爲神　朱子謂蘇氏失之

又

衆人之死爲鬼而聖人死爲神非有二致也志之所在者異也愚謂精聚則魄聚氣
聚則魂聚是以爲人物之體至於精竭魄降則氣散魂游而無不之矣降者屈而無

形故謂之鬼游者伸而不測故謂之神人物皆然非有聖愚之異也

陰精氣爲物精與氣合而生者也遊魂爲變則氣散而死其魄降矣

屬如氣之呼吸者爲魂魂即神也而屬乎陽耳目鼻口之類爲魄魄即鬼也而屬乎

爲鬼一氣即陰陽運行之氣至則皆至去則皆去之謂也二氣謂陰陽對峙各有所

以二氣言則鬼者陰之靈也神者陽之靈也以一氣言則至而伸者爲神反而歸者

又

人以爲神便是致生之以爲不神便是致死之

又

若聖賢則安於死豈有不散而爲神怪者乎如黃帝堯舜不聞其既死而爲靈怪也

又

問鬼神便只是此氣否曰又是這氣裏面神靈相似

又

銖問陽主伸陰主屈鬼神陰陽之靈不過指一氣之屈伸往來者而言耳天地之間

陰陽合散何物不有所以錯綜看得曰固是今且說大界限則周禮言天曰神地曰

祇人曰鬼三者皆有神而天獨曰神者以其常常流動不息故專以神言之若人亦

自有神但在人身上則謂之神散則謂之鬼耳鬼是散而靜了更無形故曰往而不

反又問子思只舉齊明盛服以下數語發明體物而不可遺之驗只是舉神之著者

而言何以不言鬼曰鬼是散而靜更無形故不必言神是發見此是鬼之神如人祖

考氣散爲鬼矣子孫精誠以格之則洋洋如在其上如在其左右豈非鬼之神耶

又

上蔡云我之精神卽祖考之精神

又　人物之性

釋氏之識神乃是心之妙用

又　理氣總論

性只是理不可以聚散言所謂精神魂魄有知覺者皆氣之所爲也故聚則有散則

無

又　五行

氣之精英者爲神金木水火土非神所以爲金木水火土者是神在人則爲理所以

爲仁義禮智信者是也

化書

太上者虛無之神也、天地者陰陽之神也、人蟲者血肉之神也、其同者神、其異者形、

又

太虛一虛也、太神一神也、太氣一氣也、太形一形也、命之則四、根之則一、守之不得、舍之不失、是爲正一、

柳宗元監祭使壁記

聖人之於祭祀非必神之、蓋益附之教焉、事於天地示有尊也、不肅則無以教敬、事於宗廟示廣孝也、不肅則無以教愛、事於有功烈者示報德也、不肅則無以勸善、凡肅之道自法制始、奉法守制由御史出者也、

朱子全書　禮三祭

觀此則天不可祭、而土神在民亦可祭、又雖曰土神、而只以小者言之、非如天子所謂祭皇天后土之大者也、

中國性理論與道佛之書多大不相合、即一書亦自相矛盾、言神爲本、言神爲末、皆可者不能執一而定論也、觀下三條可證、

鶡冠子

氣由神生、道由神成、

又　陸佃解天受藻華句

天受道之英華以生神明、
又

賢生聖聖生道道生法法生神神生明神明者正之末、

神吾神也從外來乎哉

老子居位篇

其神乎心神舍也舍廬而神中居心之中又有心也即性宗是　又此之謂內德註、

心之中又有心　註明亂之心中又有靜正之心也　又心官思所以爲思非心也、

管子心術下

以道蒞天下其鬼不神、註以道德居位治天下則鬼不敢見其精神以犯人也、

又漢高誘淮南子註老子曰以道蒞天下其鬼不神此謂俱沒也、

神爲生氣之浩然有深情集句

神者生之本也

凡人所生者神也　史記

神者氣也

精氣謂之神

神者道德神氣發於性也

康若樂流謂之神

奕奕有神

無限太息之神盡在其中

神高馳之邈邈　楚辭

只一語而寫盡撫膺扼捥之神

千歲後精神猶富眷戀於此　漢高祖

神字深於靈字集句

夏爲清臺何明明相承太平相續故爲清臺殷爲神臺周爲靈臺何質者具天而

王天者稱神文者具地而王地者稱靈　太平御覽

仰觀於天文俯察於地理是故知幽明之故　易繫辭

神者智之淵也

聖人謀之於陰故曰神

560　559　558　557　　556　555　554

聖人探頤索隱　註雜神道之幽密未來之吉凶坐可觀也、　易繫辭

神而明之存乎其人　註必以人心之神契合乎易之神然後鼓舞而不自知此

所謂神而明之也　易繫辭

聖人以神道設教　註聖人退藏於密　又神則無形者也　又明則有禮樂幽

則有鬼神　易象上傳

靈字集解

書經

惟人萬物之靈　註聰明亦靈也聖人先得我心之所同然而爲靈之靈者耳、

列子湯問編註

近世人有言人靈因機關而生豈謂物無神主也斯失之遠矣、

鶡冠子

神靈威明與天合　註神之精明曰靈、

字典註

佩文韻府

大雅靈臺靈傳神之精明者稱靈

567　566　565　564　563　562　561

靈字註神也善也巫也寵也福也

康熙字典

謚法亂而不損曰靈死而志成曰靈不勤成名曰靈死見神能曰靈好祭鬼怪曰靈

極知鬼神曰靈

大戴禮

陽之精氣曰神陰之精氣曰靈

咫聞錄

蠱多靜靈多祅自古爲然

又

是神也何待友則靈而自處則昧也

韓魚芍藥歌

嬌癡婢子無靈性

朱子全書　人物之性

又

故人爲最靈而備有五常之性禽獸則昏而不能備

至於獼猴形狀類人便最靈於他物只不會說話而已、

又　性理性

道無方體性有神靈此語畧有意思但神靈二字非所以言性耳、

又　鬼神

以其靈而有知有覺而言故謂之魂魄、

又

以二氣言則鬼者陰之靈也神者陽之靈也、

又　禮一

魂魄是形氣之精英謂之靈、

又　性理心

此心至靈細入毫芒纖芥之間便知便覺六合之大莫不在此又如古初去今是幾千萬年若此念纔發便到那裏下面方來又不知是幾千萬年若此念才發便也到那裏這箇神明不測至虛至靈是甚次第然人莫不有此心多是但知有利欲被利欲將這箇心包了起居動作只是有甚可喜物事有甚可好物事一念才動便是這箇物事、

579 578　　577　　　576　　　　575　　　　574

又

某按心無死生則幾於釋氏輪廻之說矣天地生物人得其秀而最靈所謂心者乃夫虛靈知覺之性猶耳目之有見聞耳在天地則通古今而無成壞在人物則隨形氣而有始終知其理一而分殊則亦何必爲是心無死生之說以駭學者之聽乎

又大學　明明德註

明德者人之所得乎天而虛靈不昧以具衆理而應萬事者也　虛無欲也　靈有覺也

又　鬼神

今廟宇有靈底亦是山川之氣脈聚處久之被人掘鑿損壞於是不復有靈亦是這些氣過了

又

愚聞錄朱子曰神之靈由於民之誠而結成之非眞有神也一人向脊則靈亦散

莊子　天地

知其愚者非大愚也大愚者終身不靈　注靈曉也

楚辭國殤　身既死兮神以靈魂魄毅兮爲鬼雄